THIRTEENERS

THIRTEENERS

Why Only 13 Percent of Companies
Successfully Execute Their Strategy
—and How Yours Can Be One of Them

DANIEL F. PROSSER

GREENLEAF
BOOK GROUP PRESS

Published by Greenleaf Book Group Press
Austin, Texas
www.gbgpress.com

Distributed by Greenleaf Book Group

For ordering information or special discounts for bulk purchases, please contact Greenleaf Book Group at PO Box 91869, Austin, TX 78709, 512.891.6100.

Design and composition by Mark Gelotte www.markgelotte.com
Cover design by Mark Gelotte

Cataloging-in-Publication data is available.

ISBN: 978-1-62634-159-3

Part of the Tree Neutral® program, which offsets the number of trees consumed in the production and printing of this book by taking proactive steps, such as planting trees in direct proportion to the number of trees used: www.treeneutral.com

TreeNeutral®

Printed in the United States of America on acid-free paper

15 14 15 16 17 18 19   10 9 8 7 6 5 4 3 2 1

First Edition

This book is

Dedicated to my father

David Capps Prosser

who challenged me to make my voice heard
and make a difference in the world.

I am grateful for your stand Padré.

*"Yesterday I was clever,
so I wanted to change the world.
Today I am wise, so I am changing myself."*

— Rumi

Table of Contents

SECTION 4 – THE BLUEPRINT FOR BUILDING A THIRTEENER COMPANY

Acknowledgments

*"Tug on anything at all and you'll find it connected
to everything else in the universe."*

– John Muir

It seems almost a cliché to say that no book is written by a single person. No one ever goes it alone, and that especially applies to me. Over the years of working to express myself through this book, many people have touched me and helped me see that the work I do impacts others. In the process, I've experienced a profound connection both with my inner self and with those around me.

I am deeply grateful to my best friend, my partner in life and business, my amazing wife, Abigail Prosser, for being incredibly supportive, curious, and engaged in my work and inspiring me to take it further than I ever would have on my own. I'm in awe of you.

Of course, there are many others: my closest friend, Dr. Susan Ellison, DDS, who for more than twenty years has listened so closely to me; my good buddy Rob Longenecker, who kept encouraging me when the chips seemed down; Bill Ferguson, who insists I can't fail—at least not now; Dr. Harville Hendrix and his amazing wife, Dr. Helen LaKelly-Hunt who have inspired me personally, in my work with clients, and through Imago Relationships International, in my relationship with Abigail.

I also profoundly thank Mitzie Hoelscher of Gap International, my coach and a decades-long personal friend; and Kent Blumberg, who stayed on me to get this work done.

Then there's my amazing family: my daughters, Katie Myler and Julia Maass, who are in my heart every day; their tremendous spouses, Monty and Tim; and my grandchildren, Grace, Ella, and Colton. I bow to the memory of my mother, Margaret Jean Prosser.

All she wanted was for me to be great. I've made some modest gains in that direction.

There may be authors who can write a book and toss it over the wall to the publisher. That didn't happen here. I relied heavily on Doug McNair and his wife, Paula, of Fleming Editorial in Minneapolis, Minnesota, to understand and clarify what I wanted to communicate. I couldn't have done it without you both. Thanks also to the very brilliant Joan Tapper, Greenleaf's editor who edited the original manuscript with a commitment to help me give the reader a quality book. Every author should be so lucky.

Finally, I thank my clients over the years—you know who you are—for your contribution to the development of this work. Your results through the test of time are my greatest reward.

Foreword

Harville Hendrix, Ph. D. and Helen LaKelly Hunt, Ph. D.

Since our expertise is in relational psychology, and more specifically, in couple's therapy, we seldom receive a request or opportunity to write a foreword on another topic. Nor do we usually accept such requests, since doing so would put us outside the bounds of our competence and our views would be mere opinion.

But we could not turn down the honor and opportunity to write the Foreword to THIRTEENERS, not because we have competence in the world of business but because the author has invited us into a stimulating, provocative conversation about the intersection of the world of business and relationship science. In addition to being our dear and great friend, and sometimes consultant, Dan Prosser's intelligence, successful experience in his craft and his wisdom make him a "source" thinker. His views could have a transformative impact, not only on the world of business, but also on a society in radical need of a value transformation.

Although we are not historians, nor do we have proficiency in economics, as relational psychologists, we do look at things historically. So we will set our comments and the author's thesis in a world historical context to amplify its significance and to show its relevance to the larger human situation; we will make some psychological observations.

But first we will define our terms. Since Prosser proposes a value transformation in business, we define the "value system" and offer four comments about how they function in a culture, like western civilization and its subcultures, business and education.

First, we view a value system as a core belief, and a set of behaviors consistent with that belief that a culture deems essential to its survival. A culture, therefore, at its most basic level is the expression of a value system. Second, since a culture consists of social institutions, like business and education all institutions of society are embodiments of that value system. Third, to change a culture it is necessary to change the value system operative in its social institutions, like business, education and religion. Finally, a value system tends to change when it no longer serves the core need for survival.

Now we create a short mosaic of value system transitions in the history of western culture. To the best of our knowledge, cultural historians have identified only three value systems in the cultures and economies of western civilization and the cultures upon which it is based. The hunter-gatherers constituted the first human culture. Since the concept of ownership did not exist then, the land and all its resources were shared by small bands of bonded couples cooperating in the search for food and shelter. The survival of the tribe was their primary value; it was ensured by an ethic of cooperation and sharing. Commitment to this value system served these nomadic/foraging societies for about 1.8 million years.

About 11,000 years ago, hunter-gatherers settled down into villages and began to raise crops and breed animals, giving birth to the experience of ownership and the development of the concept of property. Eventually, property ownership and power were co-opted by the authorities, beginning with the husband, eventually giving birth to the monarchy as a new value system. The monarchy replaced the tribe as the primary value system, because the monarch's power was connected with the survival of realm and the welfare of the individual. Since property had to be protected and more acquired to consolidate power, a social and economic hierarchy was developed, beginning with the husband who owned his wife, children, houses, land and animals. As settlements became villages, then towns and cities, and eventually nation states and empires, like Egypt, Greece and Rome, the hierarchy evolved from the husband to the village elder, to the mayor and eventually to kings and emperors. To preserve and acquire property in the form of land, animals, people and other territory it was deemed necessary for the survival of the tribe, the village, and eventually the city and empire, the only appropriate action of the subjects was "obedience." Obedience was owed to the husband who owned his wife, children, land, animals, and grain and eventually slaves; the husband owed obedience to the tribal elder who controlled the village, and eventually to kings and emperors. In this vertical political and economic structure, monologue was the structure of all conversations. Listening was not yet a cultural practice. The flow of information and opinion was one way, from the monarchial authority down to the lesser privileged.

This continued into the High Middle Ages when a slight shift occurred in the distribution of land by the monarchy to the elite, but not in property ownership as the value system. In the feudalistic society, consisting of manorial land worked by serfs, not even people, including the elite, belonged to themselves. Everyone belonged to the patriarchy, the authority above them, and the entire chain belonged to the absolute monarch of the realm, a vertical system of absolute authority that began to be eroded in the 15th century.

The erosion of the monarchy as absolute authority began in the 15th century with scientific discoveries that established new views of the universe, the rediscovery of Greek philosophy which threatened to replace faith with reason, the fight for religious freedom with the rise of Protestantism, and the political revolutions that dethroned monarchs and gave birth to democracy. This direction was fed by the rise of a merchant class, the development of an exchange economy based on money, the expansion of trade and the industrial revolution. All these momentous events lead not only to the weakening of the hegemony of monarchy, but also to the unraveling of the medieval synthesis and the shift from feudalism towards capitalism.

In the midst of all these radical cultural and economics shifts, a new construct emerged called the "individual." This individual belonged to him/herself and its preservation and enhancement became the new value system of the western world, replacing the monarchy. The features of this individual were derived from Newton's view that all objects in the universe are separate and self-contained, Darwin's view that the capacity to adapt to one's environment was essential to survival, and Freud's view that humans were instinct driven organisms obsessively seeking satisfaction of their desires. These features add up to an "individual" who is autonomous, independent and self-sufficient. Such a creature was a radical contrast to the former reality of being a "subject" of the monarchy. Instead, the isolated self became the new authority and almost all institutions of western culture have been created to protect, serve and support his needs, especially the world of economics.

Given the individual was now on his own, no longer under the protection of the monarchy nor the economic security achieved by slavery and serfdom, this autonomous self had to compete in a world of uncertainty, and thus was born the behavioral expression of the cultural value system based on the individual: competition. Winning became the game, profits the bottom line, and de-humanization of leader and worker the outcome.

Into this economic world comes Dan Prosser to study businesses that succeed and those that fail. The effect of his study is the identification and challenge of the 250 year-old economic and cultural individualistic value system that is responsible for the failure of 87% of businesses to reach their objectives. The individual, as the core of this value system, is isolated and self-engaged in competition, control and domination for its own self interest.

What the author offers as a radical and new alternative for the business world is a trilogy of relational behaviors—cooperation, collaboration and co-creation—that express a new "relational value system". To put these behaviors into action requires a shift in conversation from monologue, which is the core feature of the competitive individual, to dialogue, which is the core feature of a relational value system. When the primacy of relationship, as a fourth value system, is operative in a business, everyone involved engages in connecting conversations that create safety and a felt sense of belonging. Their interaction is characterized by cooperation, collaboration and co-creation. And they are the 13% of the companies that reach their objectives.

Since all businesses are populated with people, how they interact with each other determines the character of the business and the welfare of the persons. When people are placed in an oppositional stance, challenged to be better than others with a winner take all mentality, their anxiety is aroused, their cognitive function are impaired, and the system sometimes becomes chaotic and often dysfunctional. When persons engage in connecting conversations that prioritize relationship and the welfare of all participants, they thrive and the business becomes coherent and successful.

What makes the author a "source" is that his proposal of a relational value system for business has implications for the transformation of culture itself. In that sense he participates in an emergent revolution that includes and transcends the competitive individual as the primary cultural value, thus contributing to the shift from the age of the individual to the age of relationship.

Building Connectedness

*"Vulnerability is the birthplace of
innovation, creativity and change"*
- Brené Brown

It wasn't long after I had signed the final paperwork to sell both of my technology companies to two different corporations in the same week that I realized I was likely heading off in the wrong direction with my career. As I'm sure others who have sold their businesses have found, working for a newly "mashed up" or successor company doesn't always work well for a die-hard entrepreneur who wants to play a much larger role in changing the culture of business.

It took some serious reflection over the several months following that to discover what I was truly committed to: **"the possibility of a world where people love what they do and have what they want in every dimension of their lives"**. But then how was I going to fulfill a goal that seemed as impossible as this one?

The commitment felt a bit overwhelming to me and it didn't take long for me to realize I had way more questions than I had answers. But what really kept nagging at me was this one question: What is it within a certain few companies that make them stand apart from so many others that struggle to execute their strategy, grow rapidly, keep turnover low, become icons to their own employees?

Thirteeners, is the opportunity for me to share what I believe is the single most important quality that needs to be embraced by business leaders who care not just about income and profits but also about the impact they have on others - their employees, suppliers, customers, family, and the world.

I truly believe that of all the factors that impact the success of businesses, 'connectedness' is the one element missing in the majority of today's organizations. If today's leaders actually focused on building the connectedness their employees crave, they would see a many-fold increase in performance and bottom line results. Connectedness isn't just a value; it's a way of life for some organizations. And yet it's somewhat of a foreign concept in our business culture today.

What would you say your employees most want from their experience of working for you? Would you believe it if I told you connecting drives their desire to be a part of your team (or not)? Then would you believe me if I told you that love was the principal feeling that makes working for you worth it? People will leave your company to find the love they are looking for - that you're unable to provide.

Now, in business we generally don't talk much about love. It's too bad this is such a taboo subject. If you were to ask the employees of top companies—specifically the *Thirteeners,* who are among the top performers in their industries—you would learn the presence of love is the real difference between them and all the others. Of all the rules, principles, and values that define a company, love is the one feeling that rises above all others and makes the difference in their culture. Yet it's also the one topic that makes leaders the most uncomfortable. It's definitely time to change this reality.

I think you can at least understand when I say that we as humans crave connecting with other human beings. Then why isn't this a major issue or topic that businesses explore when seeking to improve performance? Perhaps it's because most people don't know how to talk about it. After all forming connections is an art. Yet, when connecting is practiced well, the bottom-line results can be astounding. I can't wait to share all of this with you.

I have some ideas about why leaders tend to resist the notion of expressing love in the form of connectedness and how to transform it.

And yet to say that no one is talking about it would be wrong. Actually there are several people and programs pointing in this direction... but it seems too few leaders are paying attention.

"Best Place to Work" Companies Succeed Through Conversations That Build Connectedness

By the time I finally sat down to write *Thirteeners* I'd been studying the subject of business performance for the better part of forty years. During that time, I've observed that those few leaders of companies that are truly successful in motivating their employees to achieve breakthrough results are also those frequently acknowledged as "Best Place to Work" companies. On average, experts say, these firms achieve two to three times greater bottom-line results than those companies that are not Best Places to Work.

In 2002 I had the good fortune to get my hands on two years of employee surveys of the companies competing for Best Place to Work status in Houston, Texas. In reading the responses to these surveys, and in referencing my own employee interviews at Best Place and non–Best Place companies, I began to see that the greatest differentiator between the two types of companies was not in what some experts commonly refer to as "engagement." Rather, it lay in the important conversations each company focused on and managed well.

In practice, however, it's not the conversations per se that make the difference. The conversations are simply the measure of something deeper going on: again, that elusive quality called connectedness.

In Best Place companies, leaders were clearly focused on specific conversations that connected employees to each other, to their leaders, to their organization's vision, and to their marketplace. In non–Best Place companies, employees complained about those same kinds of conversations and felt disconnected by the way those conversations were managed.

The challenge of building a Best Place to Work company isn't getting employees to be more "engaged" in their work but in understanding the true nature of human interaction and the key to success: connectedness.

If you're a CEO or senior business leader with the potential for impacting the lives of others I'm inviting you to become deeply interested in the role you play in driving connectedness into your organization. I don't make this invitation lightly. I actually implore you to learn about how connectedness and the lack of it – disconnectedness – play a critical role in your employee's workplace experience and ultimately the successful execution of your vision. Heck, connectedness actually plays a key role in the primary design of your strategy – even before you have a chance to take action on it. Overall, I'm convinced its connectedness that is going to determine whether you make the kind of numbers or outcomes that are truly possible for you and your business.

Leading the Conversations That Build Connectedness

Recently, I was introduced to the work of Dr. Brené Brown, a University of Houston researcher who has compiled and documented her own observations about the workplace, confirming and validating what I have been talking to audiences and clients about for the past thirteen years. Her principal message is this: If you want an organization that produces breakthrough results and leads your industry, you must confidently lead the conversations that will bring connectedness to your company and give real meaning to the work your employees are doing.

From where I stand that means being courageous enough to be vulnerable.

For the most part, we've come to believe that being vulnerable is not a value that pays. According to Brené Brown, women business leaders are taught that they must be perfect, while male business leaders are urged to be strong, to show no emotions[3]. But without vulnerability, the connectedness within your organization will be stifled, and without connectedness, the majority of companies fail to execute their strategy and fulfill their vision.

If you want to make your vision of a bigger future a reality, it's time to stop playing it safe and begin to explore what it means to embrace your vulnerability. Your employees will thank you for it, and, even better, they will more eagerly help get you where you want to go. Vulnerability is the vanguard or leading principle in the new world of business today that allows powerful leaders to lead connecting conversations in the workplace.

In this book, I'll show you what it takes and how you get there.

Introduction:
How to Read and
Use This Book

"When you change
the way you look at
things, the things
you look at change"

-Wayne Dyer

What Is This Book About?

This is a business book written for CEOs and entrepreneurs by an entrepreneur CEO. In this book I reveal why at least 87 percent of companies
fail to execute their strategy each year—and what you must do to transform your company into one of the other 13 percent. This book is also
about the limitless possibility found in building an organization with a
culture that is connection-driven.

What Will I Do For You In This Book?

I'll introduce you to the following:

- The positive, connecting conversations that form
  what I call the **ConnectionPoints**™ of Best Place to
  Work companies and that allow those companies to
  better execute their strategy

- The negative, disconnecting conversations that
  form the **Execution Virus,** which infects many
  organizations

- The **Entitlement Virus** that causes managers to
  believe that they must spend all their time addressing
  employee grievances rather than doing what they
  should be doing—creating an environment where
  employees are happy because they contribute to the
  company's success

- The **Empowerment Virus**, which consists of positive
  conversations that can replace the Execution Virus
  and the Entitlement Virus and put your company on
  the road to success

- **The Breakthrough Solutions Framework**™ that
  includes the **Three-Legged Stool of Transformation**

that will help you turn your company into an unstoppable organization.

- **Chaos** as the great transformer of the best organizations

Finally, I will help you rethink your strategic process by helping you see how to leverage the Breakthrough Solutions Framework for your business; I'll guide you through the ConnectionPoints Promise-Based Strategy and Execution Management System process, which I developed over the past eighteen years, first in my own companies and then for select clients.

In addition to the text of this book, there are materials online that will help you through the process. These are free and downloadable at www.ThirteenersBook.com and include the Process Map (a consolidated list of questions), the ConnectionsPoints PowerPoint (for use by leaders), a Leader's Manual, the Employee Invitation, the Employee Survey, a DIY Scorecard for teams, and the Connected Leader's Manifesto.

Why I Believe It's Time for This Book

Whether you're a for-profit organization or a nonprofit, you need to be aware of the fact that more than 87 percent of all companies with a strategy fail to meet the goals of that strategy each and every year. These aren't my numbers. According to most business experts (Robert Kaplan, Peter Drucker, and others), it's actually approaching 90 percent or more. The problem is rarely the strategy, although that is where most business leaders spend their time looking for problems when their business isn't working. I've never seen a strategy that made money for its planners; the only thing I know that makes money is a *well-executed* strategy.

This book, then, is about execution of strategy. More important, it's about who you must be as a leader to build the kind of organization where your employees will reliably help you execute your strategy.

How Should You Read This Book to Get the Most Out of It?

I'm asking you to bring a certain way of thinking—a new mind-set, if you will—to this task. I want to introduce you to the thinking behind companies that stimulate a sense of limitless possibility in the workplace to assure execution of their strategy. And what you're going to learn is that limitless possibility is a notion that any organization can thrive on.

You also need to know that what kills the notion of limitless possibility is the "disconnection" within your workplace. The biggest disconnector in business is the behavior I call "unilateral knowing," the rigid and narrow belief that you (the leader) must know the answer to any and all issues. In that case, you kill off any other possibility, which leaves you with only one course of action—the one you think you know.

Real Leadership Versus Playing It Safe

Most companies are unable to execute their strategy because their leaders have a habit of playing it safe. It takes courage to be so vulnerable that you can walk into a meeting and engage others in an authentic inquiry to uncover real solutions. What does it feel like to listen as someone twenty or thirty years your junior offers a valuable insight that wasn't even on your radar? How do you respond? Do you say, "That's not how we do it around here" or "That's not good enough"?

Well, it's those comments that disconnect the organization from you and your employees from each other. Those responses tell your employees that maybe they aren't as valuable to you as they might have thought (when, possibly, it's your own worth that took the real hit). Pretty soon, after hearing those responses again and again and having their contributions rejected, employees will leave. With them will go your best chance at gaining the breakthroughs and innovation you've been looking for all along.

The cure for this lack of connection is authentic leadership, which means uncovering the assets that others possess and that can be expressed in ways that you never before thought of. And to be an authentic leader, you must be willing to be vulnerable. I can't stress that enough. This distinction is what sets great companies apart from the merely good ones. These are the things I want to talk to you about in this book.

Embracing Vulnerability Is Leading Out Loud

In business, we experience some of our greatest victories, but we also are forced to face many of our greatest fears. I've never known it to be any other way. How we handle those fears determines our success as leaders and, to a greater extent, our employees' success. Will they feel connected to your business and to you? If your organization is to succeed, they must. And to achieve that, you as a leader need to be able to embrace your vulnerability.

Resisting the vulnerability that it takes to authentically lead today is a virtual guarantee that you'll struggle to get your company where you want it to be. I call being vulnerable "living life out loud," and if you're being vulnerable while leading a business, that's "leading out loud."

Authentic leaders lead out loud by displaying their vulnerability and by asking for and accepting input from their employees so that everyone can contribute to and "own" the company's strategy for the future. For many leaders it's scary to let employees see that you don't have all the answers, but if you want them to commit to making your organization unstoppable, it's critical.

When people feel they belong to something bigger and more meaningful than themselves, they jump at almost any opportunity to contribute. They will voice their views, add their suggestions for innovation, and offer anything else that will improve "their" organization and help it exceed even your expectations. However, when people feel excluded—for example, if they're not involved in planning the work they are going to perform—they typically fail to care. Letting employees contribute to their organization's business strategy is the single most important connector in your management arsenal.

Your job as reader of this book (yes, I'm assigning you a responsibility) is to discover in it the possibilities for your business—both for your workplace and your marketplace. You must then share those with your employees and let them contribute, as co-creators, to a strategy you can successfully execute together. This book is intended to be the start of that process.

Why Did I Write This Book and Who Is It For?

I'm sharing this book with you because I suspect that you are like me. I have started several companies of my own, and I have spent countless years trying to understand why some companies truly become great and others struggle to barely make it. This book is the culmination of many years of practical research: on how to make a difference with my clients in the hospitality industry, on what would help my employees be more satisfied in their work, and on Best Place to Work companies.

For the past decade I've helped other CEOs implement my innovative solutions to their challenging problems of strategy execution. I have seen the Breakthrough Solutions Framework work not only for me but also for others time and time again. It can work for you, too, if you're willing to step back and embrace a new perspective *for* the possibility of your business.

This book is intended for

- *CEOs* who can't get everyone on their team to align in the same direction.

- *Senior executives* who are losing team members, possibly to competitors, and who can't find the source of the dissatisfaction that is driving people away.

- *Sales managers* whose teams are not meeting quotas and who don't understand why competitors' sales are soaring.

- *Entrepreneurial partners* who have grown their start-up to some success but who can't discern the source of their inability to get everyone on their team to execute the strategy that they're certain will take them to the next level.

- *Nonprofit executive directors* who struggle with engaging a diverse board and who can't see the source of their underachieving fund-raising over the past several years.

If you're an already successful CEO, business owner, entrepreneur, professional, or leader with a compelling vision for the future—or if you're struggling to become a leader and build the business you've always wanted—I've written this book to help you:

- Understand what it will take to transform the connectedness in your organization so you can achieve your next level of performance,

- Create a workplace environment that supports your vision and that assures participation by everyone on the team, and

- Produce breakthrough results this year.

It's a Brand-New World; So Don't Get Comfortable!

In the pages that follow you will explore what it means to become a transformational executive, a leader who has the guts to lead in a way that may not feel at all comfortable at first. It may never feel comfortable. But if you want to authentically lead a powerful team of people, you need to rid yourself of the notion that your purpose is to have a comfortable time of it. You can let go of that nonsense right now. It's not going to happen.

This is not the world your parents grew up in. Once all you had to do was start a business, and the world would often beat a path to your door. You had a career you stayed with all your life. If you were an accountant, you remained an accountant. If you were a carpenter, that's what you always did. Few people broke ranks and started a company to test their ability to build an enterprise.

Companies fueled by diverse thinkers, diverse backgrounds, and diverse ideas had no place in your parents' work experience. Management was based on command and control, and it was important that everyone think pretty much the same way. In that environment, you saluted and did what you were told. There were fewer women in the workplace and you were expected to be a "company man." They gave you a paycheck, which you took home to your wife, and she put some of it in the cookie jar for a rainy day.

I'm sure I don't need to tell you those days are over. Today, each business is different. There are many ways to get where you want to go, and as a leader, it's up to you to get all of your employees to help you find your organization's unique way forward to success.

A Note About How I Use Language

To use this book, you may need to get accustomed to some unconventional ways of expressing certain concepts. I occasionally use words or language that may seem counterintuitive at first. A major part of my technology—which simply means the practical application of knowledge in an area—is the language that I use, since the entire notion of connected conversation is based on words.

For example, the future of your business exists only in your declaration: You *declare for* something that doesn't exist yet, instead of conducting a conversation *about* something you merely may be thinking about. Literally substituting the word "for" in place of "about" radically changes the context and understanding of your vision.

I want the people I work with to create conversations for something that isn't: I want them to declare for action in place of talking about action. This is a huge distinction, because it helps people in a company see that the countless hours they've spent in meetings, *talking about* what needs to happen, and thinking they were getting something done, is not true at all. What was missing was a conversation "for" something to happen. I'll discuss this in greater detail in Chapter 2.

This is just one aspect of what's different about my system, and it's necessary for transformational outcomes to take place. Futures are declared; they are not predicted.

I want you to stand in my world (as I have all my clients do) and see your business differently. That will lead to a new perspective, and perspective is everything in the new world of business. I invite you to embrace the chaos of these and other shifts in language that you'll encounter in this book.

> *"I am, by calling, a dealer in words;*
> *and words are, of course,*
> *the most powerful drug*
> *used by mankind."*
>
> – Rudyard Kipling

Connectedness and Conversations

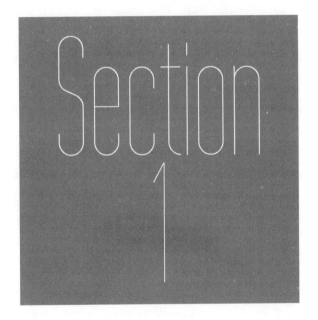

Conversations That Will Make Your Company Unstoppable

Up until now I've been giving you a behind-the-scenes narrative of why I am so passionate about this idea of connectedness and conversations. I hope you have a sense now of what's to come, as I take you through the culmination of my forty years of experience in building my own companies and helping other CEOs and entrepreneurs see a more prosperous path for their own businesses. Every consultant I know or have employed has had some kind of method or system to help put their ideas and concepts into perspective, so that they can help their clients and those they mentor through the sometimes arduous process of transforming their company into something that doesn't exist, so they can get to the next level.

For about twenty-eight years now I've been fascinated by how human thinking systems operate, both the thinking that went into them in the first place and what is driving them currently. I'm especially interested in how I might be able to impact a company's performance through a different perspective of business. This hasn't been a pastime or hobby. What drives me is a desire to see what people can accomplish when there is a shift in their consciousness, when they transform the way of thinking they have always relied on.

Here in Section 1, I discuss a concept that everyone engages in: conversations. That's a simple word to distinguish what turns out to make the biggest difference in people's performance, whether we're talking about a major company with thousands of employees or a micro-entrepreneur who works alone.

We tend to treat our conversations very casually and often take them for granted. Yet conversations are the fundamental technology of the complex evolving human system—business—that separates us from the rest of the animal kingdom. To think there might be another way of looking at the idea of conversations might seem strange at first.

Especially when we continue to use the word "conversations." But I haven't found another word that better describes this concept of language and its effect on business performance.

I'm inviting you to think differently about your conversations and the impact they have on you and others around you. Conversations are an interesting tool in your business arsenal, and when you have better mastery of the language as I use it, you will see that the world you live and work in won't be the same after you have begun to examine your own relationship to the conversations in your business.

In the next three chapters, I want to introduce you to a new world—a world of possibility that is invented through speaking. This is not what might happen if you're lucky enough; instead, this is what happens when you declare something to be possible even when you can't yet see that it really is and your past would prove you right. I have found nothing as powerful as using your voice to say how it's going to be and then have it be that way. Aristotle said that, and you can make it true.

1

How to Invent the Impossible

> "Handle them carefully, for words have more power than atom bombs."
>
> Pearl Strachan Hurd
> (British Politician, 1930s)

Declare What's Possible

Maybe it was my overactive imagination as a kid in the 1960s, but when I was in the sixth grade, there seemed to be a huge amount of fear about the Cold War. As I recall, adults didn't actually talk about the Cold War, they talked about America getting nuked by the Russians, and they taught us to deal with this frightening notion of annihilation by practicing "duck and cover" exercises in our classrooms. Looking back, it seems like an absurd experience—laughable even. Did adults really think that if we were attacked with an atomic bomb, hiding under our little desks would provide a lick of protection? Or were they just protecting us from the knowledge that if attacked, we would all simultaneously evaporate into thin air?

On May 1, 1960, the news came that the Russians had shot down an American spy plane. The pilot, Gary Powers, plummeted from 70,000 feet, bailing out at 30,000 feet right into the hands of the enemy. His U-2 plane was the most advanced reconnaissance jet we had in our arsenal at the time, but by the time Powers was going through his ordeal, Lockheed Corporation's advanced development group, Skunk Works, was already working on a new even more advanced U-2 aircraft. The U.S. government wanted an airplane that would fly higher, faster, and more stealthily than anything else in existence— an impossible airplane that nobody had ever imagined because they couldn't imagine it—and the country needed it right away.

The job of creating it had fallen to a group of Lockheed's aircraft designers led by Clarence Leonard "Kelly" Johnson, who had a reputation for producing impossible technology. But this new plane needed to go beyond the impossible. Lockheed quotes Johnson as reporting later, "Everything had to be invented, everything," He took up the gauntlet and declared that he and his team would design and build an aircraft capable of exceeding a speed of 2,000 miles per hour—and do it all in twenty months!

Kelly Johnson stood up and declared the future of aviation. Everyone else said it couldn't be done, but he stated exactly what his team would accomplish and exactly how their aircraft would perform as if it were already a reality.

The plane that Johnson and his team developed—the Blackbird SR-71—was so advanced that the paradigms of flight and aircraft navigation had to be rewritten to accommodate it. Visual references used in conventional flying were worthless to its pilots. At 83,000 feet, you couldn't see a highway, bridge, or river, so you needed to use oceans, mountains, and large lakes as reference points. The Blackbird could fly from coast to coast in under seventy minutes, and it served for more than three decades, until 1998, when it was retired due to excessive operating costs. The technology that emerged from its development has made its way into other systems that are still being used to safeguard the United States. The Blackbird now hangs in the Smithsonian National Air and Space Museum.

Though the aerospace industry was proud of its accomplishments, the people working in that industry knew that the technologies of the past were useless in building anything close to what was now needed. Given what we know about Johnson and his team, it's a safe bet that the seeming impossibility of constructing this aircraft fueled their urgent desire to create it. The Blackbird was built entirely from scratch, so it was a game changer in every sense. That's why its story is so important to your business.

Have a Conversation for Building the Possible

The Blackbird SR-71 began with a conversation *for*—not about—the possibility of something impossible, and it was fulfilled through a conversation for taking bold action. Amazing things happen when you are willing to declare the impossible to be possible—without any idea how you're going to make it so.

Everything is a function of the types of conversations you engage in. And the conversations that create every dimension of your life are the conversations that cause your business to succeed or fail. You may not think much about this day to day—after all, conversations are just words. Yet, they form your entire world. So imagine if all it took to build an unstoppable company was changing the conversations in your own life and your business. And, guess what—that's really all it takes!

Become Aware of and Transform the Network of Conversations That Are Your Business

Before your business came into existence, there was a founding conversation, and today you continue to manage your business with conversations. And while conversations appear to happen one at a time, in fact, they rarely exist as singular entities. Our day-to-day interactions are made up of interconnecting conversations.

I'll say it again: Business is a network of interrelated conversations; that's all business is. Everything you do in your business is the result of a conversation. Each business idea you come up with starts with a conversation, and each action you take as a result is another conversation.

What conversations did your business start with?	*What conversations are you having today?*	*Are today's conversations helping or hurting your business?*

There are conversations you are aware of and others you are unaware of and, as a result, pay little or no attention to. Yet those unacknowledged conversations undermine and sabotage your business; they act like a virus that infects your vision, your mission, and the strategy you're trying to execute right now. I'll discuss these in greater detail later in this book.

I first learned about these conversations more than forty years ago from a wonderful teacher—my father. I spent my early years learning about business from him. But while I knew these conversations existed, I remained unaware of their content, and just knowing about them did little or nothing for me, because I didn't have the tools to understand them.

It doesn't have to be that way for you.

Over the years, I've seen how some conversations can destroy a person's career and the quality of their lives. I've studied the conversations in poorly run, toxic, mismanaged organizations, and I've also uncovered the conversations that help build Best Place to Work companies.

I've worked with other entrepreneurs to help them see the damage they were triggering in their own organizations through their unconsciously destructive conversations—destroying trust and causing the best employees to leave.

I've seen the transformations that happen when people uncover the damaging conversations and finally begin to build what they've always wanted: a connection-driven business that achieves their most impossible dreams.

Conversations have within them the ultimate power to make things be the way you say they're going to be. Creating an awareness of conversations is one of the biggest challenges in your life and your business. At the end of the day, everything comes down to a conversation.

"First comes thought; then organization of that thought, into ideas and plans; then transformation of those plans into reality. The beginning, as you will observe, is in your imagination."

— Napoleon Hill

2

The Conversation in Which You 'Say How'

> "Ultimate power
> is saying how it's
> going to be,
> and then having
> it be that way"
>
> Anonymous

Summit Daily News
Kim Marquis

Keystone, Colorado, USA. The Keystone ski resort opened for the winter season at 8 a.m. Friday with 36 continuous hours of skiing & riding billed as the "KSMT 36-Hour Team Challenge." Two Summit County snowboarders rode away with **$3,600** in cash as the grand-prize team winners of the "Challenge." Prophetically, 26-year-old Nick Gearhart and 25-year-old Bill Pomeroy had named their team, "**The Team That Just Won $3,600.**" —November 14, 2004[4]

Inventing a Conversation on the Slopes of Keystone

You may not find it easy to believe, but every word of this story is true. I first saw it in a homeowner's newsletter and found it so fascinating that I kept it as an example for my clients to help them understand how the power of words—the conversation—determines the outcome. You, too, can build your own "Team That Just Won $3,600."

Nick and Bill had an outrageous plan to compete for the chance to split $3,600; and they actually had the courage to declare the outcome of the event weeks before it would take place. How overconfident is that?

In effect, what Nick and Bill did that day was to put a stake in the ground and declare a future outcome—a conversation they put into their team name. They decided to forget about playing it safe by looking good in front of their buddies and instead took an extraordinary risk to have something they were committed to. They were determined to say how it was going to be.

They knew they had work ahead of them, but the die was cast, and the only thing left was to follow through on what they had given their word to do—close the gap between their words and reality.

These two snowboarders had invented the most powerful conversation—a conversation to shape the future. The key to their success was their declaration of the final outcome.

Can You Do That? Or Are You Satisfied with Just Hoping for the Best Outcomes?

What about you and your business? Are you willing to put your neck on the line, to declare something that isn't, and take a stand for what you want to accomplish?

Bill and Nick, by virtue of their declaration, were already there. There was no outcome to hope for, no place to "get to." They knew what it was to cross the finish line, and they had already been there in their minds and in their hearts. It was their clarity in speaking that put them there.

If you're anything like I was decades ago, you want what you want and you have been told by everyone—parents, teachers, the media—that if you want to realize your dreams, you have to work your ass off for them. In effect, a "God helps those who help themselves" way of thinking drove me and drove my businesses: If I did really good work consistently, I believed, I could achieve what I was seeking.

Well, it's certainly possible to get through life with the hope of a big win someday. But it doesn't really work.

Then one day I realized …

Hope Is Not the Same as Possibility.

I know this will offend some people, because I have good friends who have actually written books about hope, although I wonder whether it was hope they were writing about or this thing called *possibility*.

It's easy to confuse the two. But hope is not possibility. I didn't get this message early on in my career, and it wasn't until I had been struggling in my own businesses that I realized I'd relied on a concept that undermined me. There was no creativity or innovation tied to it. Hope was not a tool I could effectively use to cause anything; it's a concept I was grabbing on to for salvation.

The best thing I could do to lead my business was to never demonstrate hope to my employees and to stop my own hoping! Hope had become an unconscious and limiting part of the culture I was creating for my companies. It had disconnected me and my employees from the possibility of taking bold action.

Today it pains me to no end when I hear anyone—politicians, clients, or TV pundits—talking about hope, and I consider it one of the most negative words in the English dictionary. In my opinion, people who hope cause nothing. They wait with the expectation that what they want will be delivered by someone else.

We've all done this without even thinking: What does it mean when you utter a seemingly innocuous statement like, "We hope to get this new client"? For me, it meant there was really nothing else to do, no action to take. It's as if I simply hoped people would read this book. With that kind of thinking my publication plans would flounder. No, I intend for you to read it and think about it—no hope involved. And I will take action to that end, because I am committed to the possibility of you loving what you do, and having what you want in your business.

Where Is the Integrity in Hope?

The simple answer is, there is no integrity in hope. I swore off hope because it didn't match what I'm committed to. This book is about using the power of your language—your speaking—to make extraordinarily bold declarations for who you say you are in the matter of your life and your business. It's about taking courageous action and producing the breakthroughs you've been looking for. That isn't possible through hoping.

Outcomes only become possible when you are willing to declare it to be possible—with absolutely no evidence that it is—and then to take the actions that are missing and that are consistent with your commitment. Your words only gain power the moment you are willing to say how it is going to be and then take the actions to have it be that way.

When I changed my language, the words I chose literally changed my perspective. When I changed my perspective I changed what was possible in my future.

Bill and Nick Didn't Hope—They Declared

Bill and Nick took the least traveled route, and they staked out their future with a bold declaration, creating a new stand for what might have seemed impossible to achieve at the time. Most people would have said it wasn't possible, but Bill and Nick said it was, and that's the difference between Bill and Nick and so many people I've encountered in business. Instead of looking at the $3,600 prize as a goal to get to, they adopted a breakthrough perspective in which they had already achieved it.

Their perspective—or their view of the future—said they didn't have to get anywhere because they were already standing there. Their stand *said how* it was going to be, and then they rode their butts off to close that gap between what they said and where they were the moment they said it. That's an amazing demonstration of ultimate power: to declare a thing to be possible as if it were already achieved and then to take the exact right actions to close that gap. That's a very powerful conversation I had to learn for my businesses and for you to learn for yours.

We All Need to Be Willing to Step Up and Say How

Bill and Nick declared their win and then took the action that made it possible. That is the kind of conversation you and your employees need now. In fact, I believe if your business could speak for itself, it would tell you, "I'm desperate for this conversation!"

When I lead performance transformation programs inside companies, I have my clients declare their outcome for the year even before they take the first step toward fulfilling it. They don't know *if* they can do it—they don't know how to do it—but none of that matters. They just know they are committed to it being that way, *and they aren't in hope about it.* They invent a conversation that says, "This is how it is right now—as if they were already there—and this is who we are in the matter of our business."

They actually stand up and say, "This is how it is right now and from now on!" For them, it's true the moment they declare it—and it can be for you, too, if you are willing to take a stand, create a bold possibility for it, believe it, and then ruthlessly and persistently stand for it and take action.

What do you hope will happen with your business?
How do you hope customers see your business?
What conversations do you hope your employees are having?
What is all this hoping accomplishing for you?

Why Should You Look at *Your* Business This Way?

Unfortunately, I've learned that the conversations in nearly 90 percent of companies are limiting, and as I've said, they undermine and sabotage your company's performance. Remember they're hidden, so you can't see or hear them, and especially because you're not familiar with how they work against you, they pass undetected through your filter.

If you can't put your desired outcome into words as if it already exists—and if you don't believe that outcome is possible—then you'll continue to struggle. To see the impossible happen in your company, you have to be willing to let go of all the notions that you have about "how it is" or "how it might not work if you take the risk." It's only that way because you say it is. You're that powerful.

Begin to *say how:* Right now, state your desired outcomes for your business, your customers, and your employees as if those outcomes already exist.

You're now at the beginning of a process that I started as the CEO of my own companies in the 1990s and then continued with other CEOs and business leaders in 2001.

As I started working with them to understand their problems, I realized that most managers are not working on the real issues or their true underlying problems; instead, they're merely tackling the symptoms of these problems.

I can relate.

I, too, had spent years addressing symptoms in my businesses: turnover, strategies that didn't work as we intended them, employees who didn't keep their promises to follow through, clients who became disappointed in our solutions to their pressing problems; issues that raised their ugly head just as we thought we were on the right path. All were symptoms of a much deeper, larger issue than most of us are trained to address. Until now that is.

I remember when things didn't go as planned; the first thing I would do is back up and re-strategize. I would look at our strategy to try to find flaws and come up with a new approach that I was sure would work this time. I took my employees through this strategy process time and time again, always thinking we would land on the perfect solution and that would be our golden ticket to the future we had in mind. I'll be honest with you; my employees got sick of this.

As I began to realize how my approach wasn't getting us anywhere, I also came to understand that solutions weren't going to be found in changing what we did or even changing the way we did it. Revising the strategy would never have provided the solutions we were looking for, because the strategy was not the source of our problems.

Our problems had their source in several things: the way we viewed our business and our thinking that resulted from the perspectives we created; the way we related to and focused on the irresolvable circumstances we faced; and the kinds of conversations we engaged in with each other that undermined and sabotaged our intentions. All of that was why we, too, were among the 87 percent of companies that struggled and failed to execute their strategy. Before we could become one of the other 13 percent, we needed to ask ourselves some pretty tough questions.

The rest of this book is about helping you, as the leader responsible for building your company, to see what is possible when you are willing to take a stand for a seemingly impossible future and then shift three critical distinctions in your business. I call these distinctions the Breakthrough Solutions Framework™. This is the structure around which I've developed the process for recovering your company and transforming not only its performance but also transforming *you* and the way you and your employees think about and relate to each other.

Transformation of anything or anyone does not happen by looking outside ourselves for insights. Transformation—true transformation —happens internally first and is then reflected externally. What you're looking for is not out there. Instead, your work needs to focus on who you are being for yourself, your employees, your clients, and for your family.

THE PROCESS
The Breakthrough Solutions Framework™

All transformation happens inside of a framework, a structure that needs to be created for a new way of thinking. It doesn't happen by chance or by osmosis. You can't read about transformation and be transformed. You have to experience it. You have to go through the process. You have to do the work.

The process I created (first for myself and then to use with clients) is designed around a simple-to-understand system—a Breakthrough Solutions Framework, a framework for transformation. This framework can be learned and applied by anyone in any organization whether he or she is a solo micro-entrepreneur or part of a giant conglomerate. The principles are the same.

At the core of the Breakthrough Solutions Framework is the recognition by an organization's leaders that they cannot close the execution gap until they:

1. Embrace a new perspective of the world and their future in it;

2. Examine their relationship to the circumstances facing them, focusing on the right challenges and letting go of those that cannot be humanly altered; and,

3. Begin to effectively manage the conversations that generate connectedness and action.

It's easy to understand isn't it? If your business is suffering from lack of strategy execution, then your current framework isn't giving you the structure you need for breaking through.

To put it slightly differently, if you change the way you look at your business, the business you're looking at will change. Just by changing where you're standing, you will begin to see things that weren't visible and available to you before.

If you stop working on avoiding the circumstances that you can't change and give up trying to avoid things like failure from happening, then you will have the energy you need to focus on causing what you do want to happen. You'll also naturally be working on the right things, those you can impact.

Finally, if you change the way you think, the way you speak will automatically begin to alter, too. We've already made clear that the conversations that you are currently engaged in and that you consistently manage—yes, manage—have a significant impact on your current results.

Add your values, beliefs, behaviors, and principles to that, and you have the overall framework for a breakthrough organization.

How Do We Get There?

Establishing a successful framework in your company requires a system, an effective process. I want to begin by helping you understand the critical principles required to be successful in the implementation of the framework.

Then, in Section 4 of this book I will teach you the process I call the "ConnectionPoints™ Promise-Based Strategy and Execution Management System." Promise-based systems are not a new concept. I first learned about them, after I had been using my own approach for some time, from the works of Professor Donald Sull at the London School of Business and business visionary Charles Spinosa.

The following chart presents these points in a more graphic format.

Five Things Missing in Most Companies

New Perspective	An enduring Breakthrough Vision of the future that puts everyone on the exact same page, an invented future that empowers people, can't be forgotten, and won't disappear or go out of existence.
	A Revelation in Awareness of the conversations and beliefs that undermine and sabotage Breakthrough Performance and a new Awareness of what is truly possible once the essential truth has been told.
A New Relationship to Circumstances	A Breakthrough Strategy that eliminates the performance gaps and the need for survival tactics and that empowers employees and other stakeholders to take responsibility for causing breakthrough results.
Conversations that Manage Connectedness and Action	A future-based Culture of Connectedness that gets the constraints left by past performance out of the way of having what you say you want and that creates the connections people need with each other and to the activities (roles/goals/responsibilities) that are consistent with the breakthrough vision.
	A Breakthrough Accountability system that gives people back their power to produce "real measurable results" using a new framework for boosting accountability to support what the organization is committed to.

"A dream is your creative vision for your life in the future. You must break out of your current comfort zone and become comfortable with the unfamiliar and the unknown"

– Denis Waitley

3

The Connection Points

"We don't accomplish
anything in this
world alone . . . and
whatever happens
is the result of the
whole tapestry
of one's life and
all the weavings
of individual
threads from one to
another that create
something."

Sandra Day O'Connor
(retired associate justice,
U.S. Supreme Court)

The Basic Model for a Thriving Business: Connectedness

As I struggled during my early years of business ownership, a new awareness stopped me in my tracks: I realized that all business is formed by conversations, and the conversations that interested me most existed inside a framework of connectedness. At the time I had actually created a framework of disconnectedness that was working against me, undermining and sabotaging my performance and that of my employees. These networks were effective at holding me back because I was totally unaware of how they worked. I knew I had to change that—and I did.

For you to gain the best results in your workplace, you, too, will need to become consciously aware of the network of conversations in your organization that impacts your employees' ability to connect and perform.

Visualize the Network

To start, it might help to visualize this network as an electrical circuit. If your organization is fully connected, power can flow through the entire network of conversations. If not, the network will cease to operate, like an electrical device with a short circuit. In the workplace, a lack of connectedness prevents the organization from creating and utilizing the power it needs to achieve its strategic plan. Even worse, the wrong connections can destroy the enterprise's ability to function properly, just as you can ruin or destroy a component with electrical power. It's the connectedness that makes the network work; this is the physics of your organization.

I used to think this idea of connectedness was just mumbo jumbo. But I eventually learned that most ancient disciplines assert that everything in the world—even things outside the physical world—is connected. It's an idea that reaches back thousands of years in Eastern thought.

When Albert Einstein came along with his theory of relativity, people in the West began to pay attention. It was about that same time that a group of European scientists—Niels Bohr, Werner Heisenberg, Max Planck, Erwin Schrödinger, Wolfgang Pauli, and others—started looking at micro-forces and objects smaller than we can see with the naked eye. They found that what we consider to be objects in fact were not. They discovered that everything is energy; things were defined only in the act of observation. (I'm grossly oversimplifying their theories because you probably didn't buy this book to learn quantum mechanics from me.)

Then, in 1964, two physicists rocked the boat by proposing that there was something even smaller than the energy and particles that the other scientists had been studying—a "God particle," as it was called in a 1993 book.[5] In March 2013 Peter Higgs and François Englert were awarded the Nobel Prize in Physics for their discovery of what's now known as the Higgs boson or Higgs particle.

What does all this mean to you and to me? Well, to me it suggests that we are all connected to everything and everyone at a deep, deep level, a level of energy never before imagined. And also that connectedness is the basic common denominator for us all.

If that is even remotely true—and I believe it is—then perhaps we could consider a new view of the way the world works and its impact on our relationships, especially those in the workplace.

I attribute many of the outcomes in business to the degree of connectedness that exists between people. Can I prove it? Not scientifically. But there are enough people who accept this view of the way the world works to make it worth talking about. Even more, it's important to implement it in our organizations so that we might realize our possibilities and so our employees can experience a level of relatedness that brings them satisfaction.

I can certainly point to my own results and the results of my clients: We have experienced incredible breakthroughs in our lives and businesses by becoming consciously aware of our connectedness to others.

Building the Connection Circuits of Your Organization

Once you can visualize your business's network of conversations as an electrical network, you can understand that several of the components operate in similar fashion. Consider that in organizations, just as within an electrical circuit, there are conductors, capacitors, resistors, and insulators.

Conductors are the power generators, the leaders who cause vital conversations to flow freely throughout the organization, knowing that the right conversation will alter the behavior of individuals and teams. Conductors might even be the champions or managers of those conversations.

Capacitors are the regulators, the leaders who gather and control the energy. They know when to compensate if the energy gets too elevated and the system is in jeopardy of overloading.

Then there are the **capacitor conductors**, leaders who exhibit both qualities. These are the great leaders in your organization because they understand how to make processes flow smoothly. They know when the right conversations are missing and when the wrong conversations have entered the system.

Resistors stand in the way of energy moving in your organization. They are the employees who become overpowered by cynicism or apathy and who struggle to adopt and adapt to the right kinds of conversations. As a result of their negative impact, they can divert energy into areas where it cannot further the strategy.

Insulators are the employees with their guard up. They are threatened by the notion that connectedness is the basic model for
business and want very little to do with all this mumbo jumbo.
I know this type of person well. They will prevent the right conversations from flowing through the organization. Insulators will often
leave the organization when the energy is turned up, because they
cannot cope with the change in the organization's direction or the
demands put on them to connect and perform accountably.

Describe a time when you have been a Conductor
or a Capacitor, or both. What was the result for
the organization? For you?

Describe a time when you were a Resistor or an Insulator.
What was the result for the organization? For you?

The ConnectionPoints™

So here's what I have boiled it all down to:

- Business is a network of conversations and a framework for connectedness.

- There are conversations in which you say how things
  will be. These are the conversations in which you state
  your vision, your purpose, what you avow as your
  values, and what you declare for the business you are in.

- There are also conversations that undermine and
  sabotage performance.

When I first became interested in the phenomenon of Best Place to
Work companies, I discovered that while most companies talk about

all the things they *do* that distinguishes them from others, that's not what makes the real difference with their clients and their employees.

What all of these Best Place to Work companies have in common is the ability to connect with the essence of what is important to their employees. These employees feel connected to each other, to their company's vision, to their common purpose, and to the company's strategy, which they can envision themselves participating in and contributing to.

Moreover, I discovered that most of these companies weren't fully aware of what made them so great. The attributes they credited for their good fortune were, for the most part, merely the symptoms of a great organization. The leadership had evidently adopted a natural "way of being" in their relationships with their employees that were much deeper and broader than they were aware of.

They were so close to the issue they couldn't see the forest for the trees. But once I understood what I thought was at the core of these organizations' success, I tested these components of workplace behavior to see if they indeed powered success. It turns out that they do.

What Is Connectedness?

It might help to make doubly sure we are on the same page about connectedness. As I've begun to share with you, who you are as an organization is largely determined by how you connect with people, both internally and externally. But how do you experience the reality of connectedness? The psychiatrist Dr. Edward M. Hallowell offers the following distinction:

> [Connectedness] is a sense of being a part of something larger than oneself. It is a sense of belonging, or a sense of accompaniment. It is that feeling in your bones that you are not alone. It is a sense that, no matter how scary things may become, there is a hand for you in the dark.

> While ambition drives us to achieve, connectedness is my word for the force that urges us to ally, to affiliate, to enter into mutual relationships, to take strength and to grow through cooperative behavior.[6]

What makes us want to enter into mutual relationships? I think it is similar to what you find in a marriage. Dr. Harville Hendrix and his wife and partner, Dr. Helen LaKelly-Hunt, have spent well over a quarter century researching this topic and have discovered that the ability to successfully create intimate partnerships goes far beyond simply wanting togetherness. The critical component is the ability to create connectedness, which supports an individual's needs to safely affiliate with others. This is true in the workplace as well. When we feel safe and passionate about our surroundings, it's then possible for fear, anxiety, and stress to be replaced by connectedness.

Similarly to the way Hendrix and LaKelly-Hunt envision marriage relationships, we can re-vision our organizations, creating safety and passion and the organization of our dreams.

Connectedness and Conflict

Hendrix and LaKelly-Hunt state that conflict in marriage is natural and expected. "Incompatibility is actually the foundation of a successful marriage," they say. The same is true for organizations. Without conflict, we become accustomed to equilibrium and try not to "rock the boat," yet without conflict (or chaos), a complex, evolving system—whether it's a marriage or an organization—withers and dies.

Diversity of opinion leads to the innovation that increases the asset value of an organization. Finding new ways to relate to each other in the workplace results in a more conscious workplace and lets us engage in conversations that weren't possible before, because we had stifled creative conflict in the past.

It's the natural inclination of the members of an organization to want to lessen or remove conflict, thinking that conflict impairs the ability of the organization to achieve its desired goals. However, eliminating constructive conflict from the workplace in an attempt to find balance and equilibrium actually destroys the possibility of finding new and innovative ways of solving problems. Please be assured that I'm not proposing heated battles in the office. Instead, I'm proposing that if you want to build an unstoppable organization, one that produces amazing breakthroughs, it's necessary to engage in debate and the defense of ideas. That is the Socratic method. Yet civil debate is only possible in an organization where people are authentically committed to making that debate safe for all others—where they are connected.

Pitting one employee against another in a way that denigrates the character of a fellow employee and bruises his or her self-image is not what I'm advocating. What I *am* advocating is a safe environment in which all people are heard, mirrored, and validated for their ideas and where those thoughts can safely be challenged. Best Place to Work companies are especially skilled at this. There's a kind of virtuous cycle in this: Connectedness allows constructive conflict and chaos, and the ensuing commitment to authentic dialogue can actually give us access to the connectedness we seek.

The ConnectionPoints™ Are Ten Connecting Conversations

While there are a multitude of hidden, disconnecting conversations that serve to sabotage company performance, there are just a handful of connecting conversations—ten of them.

The ability to manage these ten conversations between employees and managers is the best indicator of a great workplace with a culture of high performance. They shape the way people connect and help the organization produce breakthrough results.

These ten conversations are for—not about—the following:

1. Contribution

2. Acknowledgment and Appreciation

3. Alignment

4. Accountability

5. Communication

6. Relatedness

7. Responsibility

8. Integrity

9. Possibility

10. Fun, Rewards, Gratitude

As I mentioned in the Introduction, changing the word *about* to the word *for* calls people to action. Keep that in mind as we elaborate on each conversation.

The Ten ConnectionPoints™ of a Best Place to Work Company

1. **The Conversation for Being Contributable**

   This conversation gives everyone a voice in the organization. Suggestions and issues that anyone raises are taken and acted upon or resolved in such a way that each member of the organization feels he or she is being encouraged to contribute individual ideas and perspective.

   I first became aware of this conversation long after I completed my initial research into Best Place to Work companies. At that time, there were only nine ConnectionPoints. I was engaged to help a nonprofit that was struggling with growth and needed to fund-raise to support that. What I discovered was that the organization suffered from "scarcity thinking." People firmly believed that there was not enough money available in the community to help them achieve their mission. So, while their primary focus was on fund-raising, and while they were open to receiving a check to support their mission, that's where the outreach stopped. They really knew how to take the fun out of fund-raising.

People who give substantially look upon their donations as investing. Most investors I know, including myself, are very interested in the outcomes that their investments produce. In the case of a nonprofit, when I write a check, I want to do it through a relationship where they want more than just my moolah. Any organization that doesn't recognize this and doesn't develop a meaningful relationship with its contributors is going to be severely disappointed.

There is a parallel to the workplace. Employees are investing hugely of their time and intellect in going to work for you. They could be working for someone else. They want a return on their investment. Believe it or not, that return is delivered in the form of being allowed to make a difference—to contribute something meaningful to the outcome of the organization and be appreciated and acknowledged for it. I'll say more about that in a moment.

In other words, the return employees want isn't what you thought it was. The primary reason most people work for you isn't to get a paycheck. A bigger salary is akin to the better-car syndrome: When you buy a better car, you feel the pride of ownership, but soon it's the new normal; it doesn't matter all that much after a while. Giving an employee more money isn't the answer to high performance. It never has been, and I suspect it never will be. **Instead, the answer is allowing them to make a difference with *you*. Y.O.U. That's what being contributable means.**

When you're not contributable, employees will leave you for what they perceive as a greater opportunity to matter. Rarely do people leave for a salary that's only moderately better. On the other hand, when you assign responsibility and allow people to provide solutions that you actually put to use, they'll speak highly of you, and they wouldn't think of leaving. In fact, they'll want to work harder to make you even happier.

2. **The Conversation for Being Acknowledged and Appreciated**
Employees tend to adapt themselves to the reality that life is an effort. You work hard, and if you're lucky, you get ahead. We do what we do and get what we get. This is also too often the view of employees who have been wounded in the workplace before you hired them: They've been passed over for promotions and given insufficient compensation for hard work. When you hire them, it's not apparent how they have been treated in the past—and it's also not your responsibility to fix them or compensate for past wrongs. But once they've been in your workplace for a while, they may—or may not—decide that it's not all that different "here" from how it was "there." That is your opportunity to transform people's lives.

When I first realized this was an important component of Best Place to Work companies, I devised a way to introduce acknowledgment and appreciation into my clients' workplaces. Your first impression might be that it is awkward and feels clumsy, and your employees may feel that way at first as well. I promise you, however, the rewards of your effort will greatly outweigh your initial discomfort. You'll be giving your employees a gift they've never received anywhere else, and they'll feel a sense of wholeness that they've never experienced at work.

To introduce acknowledgment and appreciation into your company, start by setting a date and telling all your team members that you are hosting an Acknowledgment and Appreciation Lunch. Don't give them any details. Tell them to bring a bag lunch, or provide food and drinks if you wish.

Start the lunch with a few announcements and find some reasons to acknowledge a group or two that are responsible for some great performance. Do not allow any negative results to be discussed. This is a *positive* Appreciation Lunch, and you want it to build on what works and what is great about your organization.

After the initial announcements, hand out a sheet of paper and pen to all the participants. Ask each person to write down everything he or she would want to be acknowledged for accomplishing over the past six months—not just company matters. Tell participants they may also include things from their personal lives. For example, parents could include something about their children or their spouse, or participants could mention something they are doing to further their education. Anything is fair game.

> *What would you be proud for someone to discover about you?*
>
> *What would your coworkers be surprised to learn about you?*

Give each participant time to come up with at least six items he or she is proud of. Ask each to put his or her name at the top of the paper and hand it in. Shuffle all the papers and distribute them to the group (making sure no one gets his or her own).

Now for the fun part: It's the job of every employee to be acknowledged for exactly what he or she wants to be acknowledged for. Choose a person to start, ask him or her to stand, and then ask the person who has the chosen person's list to stand as well. Have the two of them face each other.

If you have a whiteboard, write the chosen person's name on it followed by the words "I want to acknowledge you for . . ." Then instruct the person who has the list to read what's on the board and then read the list. Then, if the person with the list knows the chosen person well, encourage him or her to acknowledge the chosen person for anything else that isn't on the list, as long as it's positive.

Odds are, the person receiving the acknowledgment will be uncomfortable. No one is used to being acknowledged. In fact, most people would rather acknowledge than be acknowledged—even though they secretly wish to be acknowledged. On the other hand, most people are willing to acknowledge if they know what to acknowledge—that's infinitely more comfortable.

The beauty of this exercise is that the person who gets acknowledged is being acknowledged for exactly what he or she wants to be acknowledged for, and no one has to guess or make up an acknowledgment that might fall short of what the chosen person wants to be acknowledged for.

Acknowledgment and Appreciation events like this will transform the belongingness in your company and elevate the endorphins people get from being singled out and told how great they are in front of everyone else.

By learning how to acknowledge, everyone starts getting comfortable with giving it away. You should plan to have an Acknowledgment and Appreciation event every month because eventually, leaders, managers, and everyone else will stop waiting until the next event to exercise their newly developed muscle of acknowledgment.

3. The Conversation for Being Aligned

Best Place to Work companies have an almost crazed desire for alignment, for everyone moving in the same direction. It's a work of art when a leader can cause alignment in an organization. In a diverse group, alignment creates energy, which is what you need to execute your strategy. To some, it might look like alignment is simply following directions. But there's more to it. You know how important it is to have wheel alignment for your car; otherwise, you feel the vehicle wobble, and your tires wear unevenly. The same is true in the workplace: Uneven alignment causes the organization to wobble and sometimes even go out of control.

In Best Place to Work companies, everyone works to stay headed in the same direction, not necessarily just by following the leader but also by making sure that when any strategic element is altered, everyone has an opportunity to contribute to changes that must take place in other areas of the business. Operations in aligned organizations have minimal confusion. There are no territorial disputes, and everyone looks out for everyone else, because everyone is in the same boat headed in the same direction.

If you're a CEO or executive leader with final authority, it's important that you use the conversation for being contributable (ConnectionPoint #1) to allow others to bring ideas to you. Your job isn't to find the holes in their concepts but to be able to say whether you can be aligned with the proposed effort or action. If you can, then you empower others to dig deep into themselves and contribute. If you can't, then share what's preventing you from being aligned. That becomes a teaching opportunity.

When people are aligned, they understand the business goals for the year and the role each goal plays. They recognize there must be alignment for their efforts to affect the bottom-line success of the company.

4. **The Conversation for Being Accountable**
   Chapter 21 is devoted to mapping and establishing accountability, so I will say only a few words about it now. When employees are being accountable, they make specific promises to take action to accomplish goals. Everyone sees everyone else's promises, and there are no secret deals to undermine the effort to keep those promises. The results of people's actions are fully measured, and everyone's contribution is visible.

5. **The Conversation for Being in Communication**
   When I first address communication with a client, it's usually near the beginning of the consulting process but

after I've measured this conversation in the Connection Points™ Employee Survey that I give them. Communication generally gets the lowest rating and is therefore the largest gap to close.

Even Best Place to Work companies struggle to shore up communication. But in companies where there is a high degree of communication, employees hear from management about anything that happens or impacts the way they do their job in a timely manner. They don't find out about it accidentally or after the fact. It doesn't reach anyone first through gossip or the grapevine.

6. **The Conversation for Being Related**

Relatedness is what I often call the source of all results. Nothing meaningful happens unless first there is a relationship. When there is relatedness, it's very easy for an employee to talk to his or her direct supervisor, because that supervisor listens. And there is real solidarity among executives, managers, and employees. If someone needs something, there is no problem with starting a conversation that gets the issue handled. This is how connectedness cures a host of ills.

7. **The Conversation for Being Responsible**

When most people hear the word "responsible," they assume it has to do with blaming others for what went wrong or for not doing what they said they would. No Best Place to Work company practices that. For them, being responsible means taking the initiative to do or cause what is necessary to get the job done. When employees are being responsible, they don't wait for a supervisor to tell them what they need to do before taking action.

8. **The Conversation for Demonstrating Integrity**

What does it mean to demonstrate integrity? It begins when management says they are going to do something, and the statement is followed with authentic action. Their actions are always in step with what they said they would do. This is not the same as being honest, decent, or virtuous. Integrity is a way of being in which management says X is going to happen, and X happens. And it applies beyond management. There is a clear and total match between what people in the organization say and their actions.

9. **The Conversation for Possibility**

This conversation means there is a future for this company. When employees can see and understand where this company is going and can feel connected to their company's plans for the next three to five years—and longer—they will not fear that their job could end suddenly through no fault of their own.

What future do you see for your company in the next three to five years?

What conversations are your employees having about the company's future?

---

10. **The Conversation for Fun, Rewards, and Gratefulness**

When your employees get up almost every morning excited and grateful about going to work and being on time (and often early), that is the greatest reward possible. On most days, employees of Best Place to Work companies can't wait to get to work. They say things like "This is a great place to work, and I feel grateful to have the opportunity to be here with these great people." Often, they say they can't believe they get to work there.

Viruses and
Disconnectors

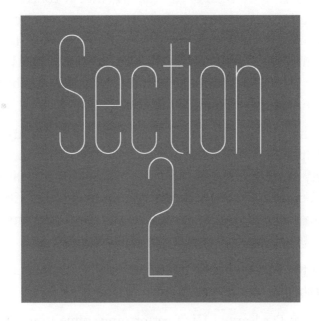

Section
2

The Hidden Viral Conversations That Undermine Your Company's Success

Let's jump from the frying pan right into the fire. In Section 2, you'll begin to see what's keeping you and your team from executing your organization's strategy. What I call execution viruses plague just about every company today. These are the disconnectors—the conversations that undermine success.

I know that disconnected companies struggle. After all, I was there once, too—ok, more than once. And whether it concerned our strategic planning, our client relationships, our innovation, the actions we took, or our results, we were either working to avoid failure, or, we were attempting to somehow leverage our strengths. Neither approach helped us get the outcomes we wanted, because something else was missing. As a team we weren't connected.

You, too, may have struggled and failed, and you certainly don't want that to happen again, so your focus is on making damn sure it doesn't. However, when leadership is focused on avoiding bad things, it can't also be focused on growth. Before you know it, other circumstances come into play, and you're not running your own company; as you will see, some other unseen force is running it for you.

Working to avoid failure is counterproductive. It results in disconnection and then in failure itself.

Here is what I've learned: High-performing connection-driven companies are positively challenged by the possibilities of a huge future. Disconnected-driven companies are being constantly tested by the small outcomes brought about by their recurring failure to execute in the past.

The future connects. The past disconnects. One thing is for sure. You're always choosing one or the other.

When I first started out in business in my mid-twenties, I was pretty proud of myself and the work I was doing. After all I was the youngest person I knew who had the guts to start a business. The truth is, my pride bordered on hubris and my ego played a huge part in causing me to overlook so much of what business is really all about. Back in those days we didn't have business coaches. But if I'd had a coach he or she probably would have given me the kind of advice I really needed. That advice would likely have been that "what I do and what I say is insufficient to make a real difference in my success."

There was another aspect to business that I never saw that would have allowed me to act in new ways. It's this: successful businesses are predicated on relationality. To be honest most businesspeople don't use words such as "relationality" even today; probably, among other reasons, because there isn't even a definition for it in the dictionary. I'm making it up. What you want and need is relationality in your business.

As you work through the chapters in this section you will begin to see that there is a relational equation to the most successful businesses. Focusing on *who I was being* would have altered the balance of things in my favor and improved my business. Best Place to Work companies innately understand this and adopt a culture of relationality—what I now refer to as connectedness. In the chapters that encompass this section, I outline for you how this *connectedness* works so that YOU, as the connected leader in your organization, can promote this thinking for your company. These are the core principles and practices of companies that exhibit the performance characteristics of a THIRTEENER.

4

The Three-Words That Undermined a Company's Success

"They don't care."

Employees, talking about management

A Tiny (but Deadly) Viral Conversation

In my early career, I built a company designed to help businesses manage their use of the new digital telecom technology that had become available after the breakup of Ma Bell. Most of my clients were hotels, which in those days resold telephone services to their guests at a fairly decent profit, if their systems were designed properly. Our job was to redesign and optimize our clients' phone business, help them take advantage of the new age of telecom technology, and run interference between our clients and service vendors (who had the advantage of understanding the technology). As we learned more about our clients and how their businesses worked, new opportunities emerged.

My company had a booth at an annual hotel technology show, and one day at a conference in San Diego my future was literally altered by an interesting conversation. A gentleman I had never met stopped at our booth to talk about telecommunications services in hotels. I think I said something to him about our most recent work—looking beyond technology optimization, at what really goes on in hotels that keeps them from maximizing profits. We required our clients to make sure their customers were not complaining about being price gouged (since customer satisfaction was fundamental to profitability), yet many of our clients still struggled with that, primarily due to lack of technology.

All of a sudden my visitor blurted out, "I know why!" Then he began to tell me a story. He had checked out of a hotel the day before, and as he looked at his room bill, he muttered something about a charge for a call that he didn't remember making.

The clerk behind the desk cheerfully offered, "Oh, don't worry, I'll be happy to take that charge off your bill, sir."

A little surprised at her eagerness to appease him, he asked, "But won't you get in trouble with your boss for doing that?"

"No," she said, "they don't care."

They don't care. Those were the most revealing words I think I had ever heard in business up until that time. I was suddenly struck with this thought: *What if even the most responsible employees at every hotel front desk had a similar conversation, saying managers don't care whether money is refunded when a guest slightly challenges his or her telephone bill?* Sure, some improper telephone charges in those days were clearly due to technical deficiencies, but for employees to spontaneously deduct legitimate charges from a client's bill at the front desk ... that was interesting and troubling at the same time.

After thinking about it and talking to others for a couple of weeks, I had a gut feeling that a conversation such as "They don't care" could be going on all through the hotel industry. If that were the case, there was no telling what other, similar conversations might be undermining the profitability of other hotel operations. What could those conversations be? I wondered. And was there was a way to fix or change those conversations, so that they would stop undermining the businesses? I decided to find out for myself.

What negative, "They don't care," conversation might be going on in your business?

What impact does it have on your customers, employees, and the bottom line?

How We Fixed the Conversation

Steve Chojnacki, the general manager at the nearby Guest Quarters Hotel, was also a good friend of mine, and I talked him into conducting an experiment on his property. Each day he would have his hotel's controller fax us the total phone charges that had been refunded to guests at the front desk the day before. We would then plot the new amount of refunded phone charges on a rolling, five-day (work-week) graph and each day fax the updated graph back to the hotel. Each day the hotel controller would tape the updated graph to the wall between the back office and the front desk. That way, front-desk personnel would repeatedly pass the graph. They couldn't avoid noticing the total refunds from the five days before and the weekly trend.

We agreed to say nothing to the employees about the experiment or the graph. That was part of the experiment. The graph simply appeared and was changed every day. No one was asked to look at it, but we made sure everyone had to walk by it.

Miraculously, the total amount of money taken off hotel bills at the front desk began to decline, and the graph began to reflect the changes. On weekends, when we didn't post a graph, the number shot back up significantly. But during the week, profits increased substantially.

All we had done was change the information that employees were observing on a daily basis, and in so doing, we changed the conversation that was running in the background. The old conversation said, "They don't care," and it was producing undesirable results. The new conversation said, "They do care." And all by itself, that new conversation altered people's behavior in a way that produced positive results.

What Are the Viral Conversations in Your Business?

What do you suppose the conversations that are infecting your business sound like? In all likelihood, negative, virus-like conversations are replicating themselves throughout your organization, and you are completely unaware of them.

These are the viral memes inside your company that are holding you back. They weaken your system of services to your clients and account for the lack of connectedness with your employees. Gaining complete, conscious awareness of them is the first step to building a breakthrough company.

In the following pages, I will reveal what negative viral conversations sound like, what they do to your company, where they come from, and how you can replace them with positive viral conversations that will make your employees able to execute your company's strategy and move your organization forward to where you declare it will go.

"Information is almost never enough to spark change. Only when information powerfully impacts the current prevailing conversation do people choose to alter their behavior. Choose your information wisely, and use it with intention"

— Dan Prosser

5

What an Execution Virus Is, What It Looks Like, and How It Infects and Disconnects Your Business

"The life I touch for good or ill will touch another life, and that in turn another, until who knows where the trembling stops or in what far place my touch will be felt."

Frederick Buechner
(writer and theologian)

In *The Selfish Gene,* published in 1976, British scientist Richard Dawkins coined or adapted the word "meme" to bring evolutionary principles into a discussion of how ideas and cultural phenomena spread. Dawkins said, "I think that a new kind of replicator has emerged on this very planet... We need a name for the new replicator, a noun that conveys the idea of a unit of cultural transmission, or a unit of *imitation*... I want a monosyllable that sounds a bit like 'gene.'"[7] He cited melodies, catchphrases, beliefs (notably religious ones), fashion, and technology as examples of memes. The Merriam-Webster dictionary defines a *meme* as follows:

> A meme (\'mēm\, *meem*) is "an idea, behavior, or style that spreads from person to person within a culture."

So a meme is a unit of transmission of cultural ideas, symbols, or practices. It facilitates the spread of such things from person to person through writing, speech, gestures, rituals, and so on. Meme theorists look upon memes as analogous to a culture's genes in that they self-replicate, mutate, and respond to selective pressures.

These theorists also hold that memes evolve by natural selection, just as organisms do. Variation, mutation, competition, and inheritance determine whether an individual meme will reproduce and how well it will do so. Memes spread by making their hosts behave a certain way, and those memes that propagate prolifically will survive, spread, and mutate. It's also critically important to note that some memes may replicate themselves and spread even when they prove harmful to their hosts. It sounds a bit sinister as I describe it. But as you will learn, some memes do threaten your future ability to grow and prosper.

The Genetic Code of the Workplace

The application of meme theory to the workplace is fascinating because just as a species' genetic code plays a role in its survival or extinction, memes—the genetic code of the workplace—play a role in the survival or failure of your organization.

Much as a flu virus might infect all employees and produce illness, memes infect the thinking and actions of entire organizations, with the creation of a network of limiting conversations, for example.

I have observed closely how memes create the genetic code of the workplace. They occur only in the context of language—of conversations. They determine what's possible and what's not possible, within the context of your strategy, for your future. You have limiting memes in your workplace right now, yet you don't know they're there, unless you know what they look and sound like. Even the most limiting memes are not visible until you find the key to discovering them.

In the workplace, limiting memes exist through a system of hidden conversations that affect which information is created, interpreted, and disseminated. These memes form what I call the Execution Virus.

The Impact of the Meme

Memes are the pathogens that enter the workplace in the form of the Execution Virus and limit your thinking and actions to what's currently believed to be possible. But when you know where to look and what to search for, uncovering the Execution Virus in your organization is relatively simple. After that, you need to understand the process of transforming it. This book will take you there.

Three Execution Viruses

Here are three scenarios that exemplify day-to-day life in companies that have been infected by an Execution Virus. Written in bold at the end of each scenario is a sentence that summarizes the hidden conversation taking place in that company, a conversation that has become a viral meme in that company—an Execution Virus.

Scenario A:

Jackie is the manager of a human resources department. She wouldn't tell you this, but she is prone to confusion, and finds that state intolerable. She wants immediate answers from her staff, because if she doesn't feel certain of something, her anxiety gets the better of her. Her behavior when she doesn't have all the answers is becoming a problem for her staff, and having to stop and handle the disruption caused by Jackie's behavior distracts the group from its purpose. Everything stops when they have to take care of Jackie's emotional needs. It's an unhappy situation, and there appears to be no solution because there's no one to appeal to for relief from Jackie's negative behavior. Her team starts thinking, **"No one cares what this woman does to our morale, and they'll never do anything about it, so we're screwed."**

Scenario B:

John is the customer service department manager, and he is very distressed. He resents the way he's being treated by his bosses, and his coworkers aren't any happier. They are offended by the rules changes that are summarily handed down from on high whenever something isn't happening that someone feels should be taking place. It's not even clear what needs to happen. Nevertheless, "they" just changed the rules again.

John just came back from an executive management meeting and discovered an email that changes procedures that have been followed for years. Customer service and support employees will now be required to get approval from two levels up whenever they want to accommodate an unhappy client. Previously if there had been a problem, call center employees were authorized to do whatever was necessary to make it right for the customer. Now it will take a week or more to process any customer complaint, and by that time, the customer will be furious.

John believes that whenever management is not happy, they take it out on everyone else, and they do it because they can't get it together themselves. It's also embarrassing for John to have to tell his team members to make these changes because they all know full well that within a month there will be even more changes. No one in top management can make up his or her mind about what to do, and no one has thought to ask the people in customer service what they think is the best solution. If management asked, John and his fellow team members would be happy to show them what's needed and how to handle the issues, but instead John and his team have started to believe, **"We're not worth listening to, management doesn't care what we think, and it won't get better any time soon."**

Scenario C:

Rachel is responsible for software sales, and she's fed up. Her most recent customer just called and chewed her out because of the problems his organization is having with the new software she sold them. The software doesn't work as promised, and the customer is running out of patience. This isn't the first time this has happened, but whenever Rachel takes a client's problems to the software support department, they tell her it's the client's fault for not saying what was needed when the software was installed.

This is the third customer to call this week with a similar problem, and the third time she's gotten grief from software support. She is struggling with her sales, and she hasn't had an interested client prospect in over three weeks. She's thinking that if she sells software to any other clients, she will just get more calls from them with more problems, and that's the last thing she wants to have to deal with. At this point, she's thinking, **"The software is flawed, management doesn't care,**

and there's just no sense of urgency from the support department to solve any of my clients' problems—I give up."

These committed employees have three things in common:

1. They care very much about what they do for their customers.

2. Each of them is experiencing the chaos of the workplace, and there's no apparent solution coming from higher-ups.

3. Each of them has been infected with a deadly and common workplace virus, a meme, that doesn't stop with them—in other words, an Execution Virus.

What similar story can you tell about a Jackie,
a John, or a Rachel in your organization?

The circumstances in these particular scenarios and the hidden conversations that result have a direct and lasting impact on the overall performance of these three employees' companies. However, what these employees think is the problem is really a symptom of a much deeper issue. No one is consciously aware of the contextual source of the problem—the conversation that's running in the background of each of these companies. They are only aware, indirectly, of the outcomes. The outcomes are visible, but the causes are not.

The Damage That Execution Viruses Inflict on Businesses

How do you think the employees at these three companies might act as a result of these conversations? I can help you with that.

Scenario A:

Jackie's HR department employees are working hard to avoid any confrontation with their drama-laden supervisor. That means they are removed from the mission of the company and the purpose of the HR department, which is to serve the company's employees and their supervisors.

Scenario B:

John thinks nothing will ever change for the better, and he's dreading having to deal with all the unhappy customers that the new rules will produce. He will find a way around the situation, or he'll pass the problems off to someone else. He will struggle to do his job and will continue to resent upper management, who apparently don't know what customer service agents have to deal with and who don't communicate with anyone at his level—except to issue edicts through the division manager. Sooner or later, a better job will come along, and John will jump at it.

Scenario C:

Rachel is done selling software. She's still on the payroll and will be as long as she can hold out, but she doesn't want to lie to prospects about the efficacy of the product and its (in)ability to solve their problems. That just creates more problems for her to deal with, and she hates getting angry calls from customers who don't get any satisfaction from the support department. She is convinced that the company doesn't care that she is faced with disgruntled clients, and she no longer finds it easy to pick up the phone and follow up on leads for new business. Cold-calling is a thing of the past for her, and she would rather risk losing her job than create additional problems that make her life more miserable. She is embarrassed to work for her employer.

The hidden conversations—and the beliefs and actions they create—aren't confined to Jackie's employees, John, or Rachel. The conversations are spreading like wildfire throughout these employees' respective organizations—replicating like a virus. The way management and others act or do not act toward them has infected everyone. These employees' beliefs, attitudes, and feelings that their organization lacks values are invading the culture of the organization, undermining and sabotaging the organization's ability to execute its strategy. This is the Execution Virus in action.

The Execution Virus Creates Disconnected Companies

As we explained in Section 1, connected companies produce extraordinary results, and companies become connected (usually without knowing it) by engaging in the ten conversations I call the ConnectionPoints. Here we see the opposite effect: Hidden, viral conversations cause employees at Jackie's, John's, and Rachel's companies to become disconnected from their company's mission and purpose, thus producing poor results. While Jackie, John, and Rachel names are fictionalized, the situations they find themselves in are not made up. Scenarios just like these take place at businesses in every country every day, and even the best companies aren't protected from the insidious viral memes that lodge themselves in the workplace and force entire organizations to settle for mediocre results or worse.

Why Does This Happen, and What Can You Do to Fix It?

You'll notice that in each of these three scenarios, the Execution Virus originated not because of something the employees were doing but because of something they were reacting to. Jackie's staff was reacting to Jackie's chronic negative behavior, John and his staff were reacting to arbitrary and damaging rules handed down by uncommunicative management, and Rachel was reacting to a lack of help from the software support department. Moreover, in each of these scenarios, the employees felt powerless to change the situation. That is another identifying aspect of a disconnected company: The employees feel powerless to make the company's situation better.

But before you as the leader of the company can address that problem, you must first discover what is causing employees to feel powerless. In many, if not most cases, the person causing that problem is right at the top—meaning it could be you. It comes down to awareness: Looking in the mirror and finding out what you're doing to cause your company to become disconnected and infected with an Execution Virus is the first step to replacing the Execution Virus with a new meme that creates a connected, successful company.

"A high percentage of organizations develop a military rationale, whereby only a very small number of people make all of the decisions. There is little wonder, then, that people aren't keen to get out of bed and come to work on a Monday morning."

— Ricardo Semler

(Brazilian entrepreneur best known for
his radical reform of the workplace)

6

To Fix Your Disconnected Company, Look in the Mirror

""The floggings will continue until morale improves."

Anonymous T-shirt

To Grow Your Company, You Must Be Willing to Grow as a Leader

I meet many business leaders who want me to help them grow their companies but who have very little authentic commitment behind their façade of hope for making that happen. What they really want from me is to "change" their employees' behavior so that they, the business owners, won't have to do what they know deep down they must do: grow as leaders. A commitment to changing others, rather than to changing one's own way of being in business and one's own way of relating to employees is not leadership but merely the pretense of it.

Frankly, spending money to fix employee behaviors in hopes of getting workers to produce better results is a waste of cash. Retraining employees is worthless if the person at the top refuses to alter the way he or she thinks. That's why you find business owners who complain that the last consultant wasn't effective and that the company couldn't sustain the results of the training. The changes that the consultant proposed never made it off the ground because there was no connection to a vision, no commitment to change leadership behavior. How do I know this? At one time, I was one of those leaders who fell for change tactics. I'm eager to save you some time and money by sharing what I learned.

Any transformative initiative in a company demands that the key leaders of the company be willing to examine their own behavior first. Only then can they start helping those who work for them formulate a better approach to executing company strategy.

A True Example of a Disconnected Company

I'll give you a great example of how poor leadership behavior creates a disconnected company. This is a true story. A close friend who wasn't sure what she wanted to do next in her career agreed to take a "temp to perm" assignment with a well-established and respected investment banking firm. You know how it works: The company and the employee try each other out to see whether the connection will work. Two senior investment bankers from an international mega-trading firm had started this particular firm in the early 1990s. The two founding partners had recognized an opportunity to capitalize on the market as it was at the time, and so they left the big firm and formed their own company. Presumably, these two highly successful gentlemen saw the opportunity to have their own firm and reap the profits of their own hard work rather than make a larger firm wealthy at their expense. However, twenty years later, although the firm had grown and was successful, it appeared rudderless and without a defining purpose.

On the first day of work at the firm, my friend learned that she was just the latest in a long succession of new employees who had joined the company and promptly left during the past five months. The job that had drawn these short-term employees was an entry-level receptionist position, and that's the position my friend had decided to take.

On her first day my friend was trained to answer the phones and make coffee for the partners. She was told not to worry about learning the conference call system, since the only conference call that day would be for the partner who set up and handled conference calls on his own. However, two hours into the morning, the switchboard lit up with four calls and then more calls. Conference callers were dialing the main number because the partner had sent the wrong code to the conferees, and no one was able to access the scheduled conference. Three other women in the company jumped in and scrambled to figure out what had gone wrong. But all hell broke loose, as the phone system was over-loaded. Suddenly, the responsible partner came storming out of his office and screamed at the new employee, "What the f--- do you think you're doing? You're giving out the wrong f---ing code to people." The four women stood there dazed.

What happened to my friend that day happens far too often. The negative behavior of just one leader set a negative tone for the culture of the entire company, and as a result, no new employee wanted to continue as a full-time employee.

But it didn't end there. My friend had been instructed that a certain partner wanted a fresh pot of coffee placed on his desk at exactly 2 p.m. each day. She noticed on the company calendar that this partner was scheduled to be in a meeting in the conference room at 2, so she made a fresh pot of coffee at 1:55 and set the new pot in the conference room as a convenience for the partner and his meeting attendees. That was all to the good; she was savvy enough to anticipate the moves of the partner she was trying to support.

Promptly at 2 p.m., the partner emerged from his office and, without looking or asking if his coffee was ready, said to her in a demeaning tone of voice, "I sure hope you are going to be brewing me a pot of coffee at 2 p.m." She looked back at him and told him that the fresh pot of coffee was in the conference room waiting for him, because she knew that's where he'd be. The only response from the partner to this initiative on the new employee's part was, "Oh." No apology, no explanation, no responsibility for his behavior or the deprecating tone that he had just subjected the brand-new employee to—and no "Thank you" either.

As you've probably guessed, my friend didn't stay in that job.

Why Do Leaders Behave This Way?

The leadership behavior described in the previous example happens every day in thousands upon thousands of companies. The boss considers him- or herself to be above the employees and therefore entitled to behave in any way he or she sees fit, regardless of the impact. That attitude of "you are here to serve me" reduces the employees to doing only one thing well: working hard to avoid upsetting the boss.

It also causes them to resent the boss every minute they're working. Far too many companies tolerate this kind of behavior, despite the fact that when employees are working to avoid unacceptable antagonism, they're definitely not working on finding ways to improve the company's value to clients or increase its revenue.

I think this is unconsciously learned behavior. Maybe the current leaders of the company were once treated that way by others, and so they think that is how all leaders behave. However, such behavior creates a major disconnect between the employees who have to endure it and the strategy that the employers want to execute. No employee thinks about how best to support the company's strategy when the focus is on surviving in a toxic workplace.

The fact that these leaders exhibited unacceptable and even abusive behavior—and that the other leaders in the company tolerated it—says a lot about the people running the company. Accountability for such behavior was nonexistent, and while the leaders' goal was to make money, they had no respect for what others in the firm were doing to help them accomplish it. The employees were focused only on making sure they didn't end up in the crosshairs of any of the spoiled-brat leaders who habitually threw little-boy temper tantrums and degraded people if everything wasn't exactly the way they wanted it.

Looking-Glass Companies

I call this kind of disconnected company a "looking-glass company" for two reasons:

1. If the leaders of the company would look in the mirror, they would see the source of the majority of their company's problems.

2. Employees reflect the thinking and behavior of their leaders.

Looking-glass companies are a common type of disconnected company, and the leaders in these businesses refuse to examine themselves and their own behavior as the source of their organization's poor performance. As a result, they will likely never achieve their full potential. A looking-glass company is essentially drifting. It goes wherever a blowhard leader decides to push it that day. If the leader is in a good mood, the employees breathe a sigh of relief that they've made it through another day. If not, there's no telling what the employees will have to endure. Far too many business owners focus on creating a company that is designed to make money, but just for them. Everyone else is chattel. This isn't a problem of excessive greed or avarice. It's bigger than any Wall Street issue; it's a Main Street problem.

I don't begrudge anyone wanting to earn their fortune by creating and building a business. That's been my life for more than forty years. The problem is that when the leaders of a business don't state a purpose or take a stand for something bigger than themselves, the company devolves into a workplace where employees are miserable. When workers resent the way they are being treated or how they are expected to work, when they get little direction and are then ridiculed when they get it wrong, they produce about 33 percent of the possible results. That's because they're not focused on producing results—they're focused on covering their asses.

To Start Fixing the Disconnect, Make Your Company FOR Something—Not Just ABOUT You

A rudderless and drifting organization like a looking-glass company isn't *for* anything. It's *about* the owner. It rarely takes into consideration anyone but the founder, or anything other than the founder's ego and financial needs.

Most entrepreneurs and CEOs I talk to say they want their company to experience double-digit growth or become a Best Place to Work company, or both, but few of them have the integrity to look at the source of the problems that cause them to fail at executing that strategy. Becoming a Best Place company takes a leader with a high level of desire and a willingness to do whatever is necessary to produce breakthrough results. That includes changing one's perspective and modifying one's own thinking and behavior. Too frequently, leaders believe that all the work they need to do on themselves has either already been done or would be a waste of time.

"When there's ever a breakthrough, a true breakthrough, you can go back and find a time period when the consensus was 'well, that's nonsense!' so what that means is that a true creative researcher has to have confidence in nonsense."

– Burt Rutan

(American Aerospace Engineer)

7

Why Your Employees Aren't Executing Your Strategy

> "If we start to look
> at companies as
> complex systems
> instead of machines,
> we can start
> to design and
> manage them for
> productivity instead
> of continuously
> hovering on the
> edge of collapse."
>
> Dave Gray
> (author of The Connected
> Company)

When I interviewed leaders from Best Place to Work companies, I discovered that while they concurred with my understanding of their organizational culture, they didn't have the language to describe it. As a result, they weren't aware of the distinction between their own Best Place to Work culture and others. This is important, because if you want to produce a breakthrough in your company, you need the language to describe the source of your results—good or bad. You also need an awareness of the hidden conversations your employees are having, because, as I've already said, the greatest challenges in business today are the unseen obstacles—those limiting and negative viral conversations that undermine and sabotage individual and team performance.

The Ten Conversations That Undermine Your Strategy

I've compiled a list of ten conversations that always obstruct performance. These conversations might well be in your organization, and you will recognize them if they are.

These conversations aren't complicated. They don't require you to have training in organizational development to recognize them. However, they are the reason your employees are disconnected from you, from your vision, from your mission, from the strategy for your company, and from the needs of your customers. They add up to your Execution Virus.

1. **"It's not our strategy."**
   There's no buy-in for your strategy because your employees have nothing invested in it—nothing contributed, nothing at stake. Your employees invest in their work, but that's it. They have no say in the direction of your company, and therefore, they disconnect and passively withhold themselves.

Employees who are not invited to the table to contribute don't see your company as their company, because they don't see your strategy as their strategy. You do all the planning, you demand a certain result; they do all the work, and you get all the reward. They are expected to invest themselves in their work and produce results, but they didn't agree to this path and they question some aspects of it. That's because you didn't ask them what they thought or how they saw themselves fulfilling their roles.

Don't talk about "engagement" and "empowerment." Do allow people to contribute to the direction of your company. This gives them a way to make an investment in what they are working on and gives real meaning to that work.

2. **"They don't appreciate us."**
Employees are resentful of management for not recognizing their contribution to the success of the organization. This is an easy conversation to overlook, and I've found it's one of the more awkward conversations most leaders struggle to address. It was for me for many years.

No matter what level of skills a leader has achieved, I've rarely found an executive who is comfortable *authentically* (meaning from the heart) acknowledging or expressing appreciation for an employee in front of others. It's rarely done in business. So many leaders believe that if they acknowledge someone, it will come back to haunt them; perhaps the employee will take advantage of the comment when the time comes to review his or her performance and salary. So leaders think, *They get a paycheck, and that ought to be enough acknowledgment and appreciation.* Nevertheless, employees may still feel exploited. It can cost you big-time not to have that conversation. It costs you nothing to appreciate and acknowledge the contribution of others.

3. **"They're always making excuses."**
   Employees learn from their leaders. When leaders use ready-made excuses, point the finger of blame at peers or other team members, or point to circumstances beyond their control as reasons for failing to deliver, employees will find their own excuses for not doing what they said they would do. This produces a business culture in which strategies, plans, and intentions disappear soon after they are agreed to, and teams quickly fall back into business-as-usual behavior. No one holds management accountable, because that just isn't done. The underlying message from management is, "You're in no position to question me as to why I didn't do what I said."

4. **"Did you hear what (Team Member A) said about (Team Member B)?"**
   Gossip and stories that degrade others in the organization create a bullying and toxic workplace environment. If your employees are experiencing the scorn of another employee, or if management knowingly tolerates gossip about others, then you have employees who will give just enough to get by.

How do you know a conversation is gossip? If what is being said about another person can't be said to someone's face, it's absolutely gossip. Wherever there are secrets or anything that cannot be discussed at any level of an organization, you will find a dysfunctional organization that's unable to focus on what matters. There is no alignment with what is important, because people feel bullied.

5. **"What mission statement ... and why should I care?"**
   Sit everyone down unannounced and go around the room.
   Ask them to tell you the mission or vision statement of
   your company. If you're lucky, maybe 5 percent of them
   will be able to give you an answer. As for the rest, you'll
   have difficulty getting them to understand the relevance
   of the company's mission and getting them to implement
   it with any sense of urgency. How can people implement
   actions or execute a strategy when they can't understand
   the relevance of your vision and mission and connect it to
   their job?

6. **"They treat us like shit."**
   If there's mistreatment, rudeness, and nastiness toward
   employees, leaders will surely take action to stop it,
   because they know that no company can execute its
   strategy with that going on, right? Apparently not. In a
   study that spanned fourteen years, Christine Porath and
   Christine Pearson found that 98 percent of employees
   they surveyed reported experiencing rude or uncivil
   behavior either toward them or toward another.[8] In 2011
   alone, half of employees surveyed said they were treated
   rudely at least once per week. That's a 100 percent increase
   since 1998, when only a quarter of employees reported
   rudeness at work. What gives? Evidently quite a bit.
   Uncivil behavior hits squarely at the bottom line, because
   those who are on the receiving end nearly always report
   responding in a negative way. The article pointed out
   that employees do their worst work under the duress of
   being disrespected, and that feeds the turnover problem
   in many companies. It doesn't just impact the workplace,
   either. It spills over to negatively impact customer relationships as well.

Here are the full effects that rudeness at work has on employees:

- 48 percent of employees intentionally decreased their work effort.

- 47 percent intentionally decreased their time spent at work.

- 38 percent intentionally decreased the quality of their work.

- 80 percent lost work time worrying about an incident.

- 63 percent lost work time avoiding the offender.

- 66 percent said that their performance declined.

- 78 percent said that their commitment to the organization declined.

- 12 percent said that they left their job because of uncivil treatment.

- 25 percent admitted to taking their frustrations out on customers.

- And worst of all, 25 percent of offending managers said they didn't recognize their own behavior as uncivil.

The researchers drew the following conclusion:

"The costs chip away at the bottom line. Nearly everybody who experiences workplace incivility responds in a negative way, in some cases overtly retaliating. Employees are less creative when they feel disrespected, and many get fed up and leave. About half deliberately decrease their effort or lower the quality of their work. And incivility damages customer relationships. Our research shows that people are less likely to buy from a company with an employee they perceive as rude, whether the rudeness is directed at them or at other employees. Witnessing just a single unpleasant interaction leads customers to generalize about other employees, the organization, and even the brand...

We know two things for certain: Incivility is expensive, and few organizations recognize or take action to curtail it."[9]

7. "It's the same old story."

Employees are becoming employer deaf. Grandiose pronouncements for new initiatives by managers today, intended to provoke a new battle cry, are falling on deaf ears. That's because employees have heard it all before. Bringing your employees together to build new initiatives for a goal or challenge is usually received with rolling eyes and sighs of annoyance and anguish.

Employees are smarter today. They can tell when leaders are inauthentic in their pronouncements. They will usually give you one chance to get it right. No one wants to feel manipulated into thinking that what you're putting forth is brand new. It rarely is. There are too many options available (even in a sluggish economy) for good people to stick with leaders who aren't serious about being authentic.

8. "Because he's (or she's) the boss. That's why."

A patriarchal and paternalistic culture exists in far too many companies. Established by leaders, this societal construct is, surprisingly, kept in place by none other than the employees. Patriarchy and paternalism are symbiotic in that they require both the leader and the led to cooperate. Although both ideas are expressed with masculine words, the concepts don't apply solely to males. They apply to female privilege as well. There are plenty of matriarchs leading companies today, but whether the leaders are patriarchs or matriarchs, a patriarchal and paternalistic business culture entails employee subordination: There are the haves, and they have all the answers; and there are the have-nots, who have no power.

Most people grow up in a solid paternalistic model of family governance, so it feels very natural to have a "decider" and a "decidee." One person has the job of saying what everyone else will do, and the rest are paid to do what they're told. But that's just a modern version of forced submission.

Employees buy into a patriarchal and paternalistic business culture because it lets them off the hook. They can avoid having to make promises and take action. Instead, they can wait until someone tells them what to do. That creates a dependency on receiving orders from leadership, and those employees can't execute your strategy because they won't take responsibility for causing things to happen.

9. **"We've always done it this way."**
   Old paradigms, nonexistent "visions," and limiting business models that are fixed on past performance keep your employees from moving your business forward. A rigid belief system that creates inflexible boundaries around what is possible for the future makes employees feel stifled. When employees can't see how or where they can improve their position in life and can't perceive a future for themselves that doesn't look and feel a lot like the past, they become apathetic.

   Employees who haven't been shown that they can grow, develop, and expand their opportunities within the organization—so that they have a sense of control over their own possible future—will lose interest in what you want.

10. "The boss is watching, so just don't screw up."
Leaders who focus on "not losing," rather than on working to build something they can share with their employees, end up sabotaging their own organization. For an employee, there's no benefit to coming to work each day for a leader whose fears dominate the working environment. Those employees just put in their time.

Leaders who are in constant fear of the unknown and uncontrollable events in their business need to get a grip. There's no faster way to turn good employees into cynical and nonproductive ones than to stress them out for no purpose other than to feel like you're controlling the possibility of failure.

"So what do we do anything. Something. So long as we just don't sit there. If we screw it up, start over. Try something else. If we wait until we've satisfied all the uncertainties, it may be too late"

— Lee Iacocca

Isolate the Execution Virus and Apply the Vaccine Of Truth

"Many people have laid down their lives for their ideas or ideology. These ideas are infectious. There are a lot of ideas to die for. Most people have been infected by parasitic ideas. . . Most of the cultural spread that goes on is not brilliant, new, out-of-the-box thinking. It's 'infectious repetitis.'"

Dan Dennett

The "Virus" That Destroys Anthills

Dan Dennett is an Oxford-educated American philosopher, writer, and cognitive scientist, currently a professor of philosophy at Tufts University. In 2002 he gave a fascinating TED (Technology, Education, and Design) talk called "Dangerous Memes."[10] It's definitely worth your time.

In his talk, Dennett explains the unique and bizarre behavior of what he calls zombie ants. He describes a natural phenomenon in which a parasite infects ants in the Amazon rain forest and turns them into automatons, or "zombies." The parasite takes over all the functions of their bodies and brains, and the zombie ants have no further control over what happens to them. Their unusual behavior, if left unchecked, could result in the destruction of the entire ant colony.

The parasite—a fungus, actually—deposits its DNA into the ant host, pretty much like a human virus does in humans. The DNA, a form of information, then recodes the host's brain to behave in uncharacteristic ways that perpetuate the life cycle of the parasite. The parasite doesn't care about its impact on its host. It cares only that its own life cycle be perpetuated.

But We're Not Ants (Right?)

So how does this apply to your business? Dennett commented that people's thinking is infected by ideas and notions in much the same way that the brain of the ant is infected by the parasitic fungus. "Many people have laid down their lives for their ideas or ideology," he said. "These ideas are infectious. There are a lot of ideas to die for. Most people have been infected by parasitic ideas."

He then went on: "It's ideas, not a fungus, that hijack our brains. Most of the cultural spread that goes on is not brilliant, new, out-of-the-box thinking. It's 'infectious repetitis.' Hosts work hard to spread these ideas to others. One set of ideas or another have simply replaced our biological imperatives in our own minds . . . It's part of how we seek our highest good . . . The biological effect of ideas [and ideals] causes us as humans to subordinate our natural genetic interest to other foreign interests or ideas. No other species does anything like this."[11]

In a nutshell, ideas can replicate through no effort on our part as they pass from brain to brain. How does this happen? Is it possible that toxic ideas could wipe out entire organizations just as a parasite can wipe out an entire ant colony?

Consider for a moment that an ant colony is like a massive business with an amazing level of intelligence when gauged on a human scale. In many ways, the colony is like *your* business, but with two major differences:

1. **"Ant strategies" get executed 100 percent of the time, on time, every time.** Ants always do what they're supposed to do, when they're supposed to do it, contributing to the smooth operation and survival of their organization and their species. Ants operate on instinct, but that isn't the same as operating unconsciously. And that is because of the second major difference between an ant colony and your business.

2. **Ants are consciously aware of what is threatening their survival; you're not.** When ants run into trouble, Mother Nature (think chairman of the board) provides them with an awareness of the source of the threat, as well as a masterful way of responding to it. Specifically, as the parasite takes over an ant's brain, the ant begins to behave irrationally. Once the other ants become aware of the aberrant actions, they isolate the infected ant, take it far away from the colony, and dispose of it.

Unlike ants, most human business leaders have absolutely **no conscious awareness** of what's preventing the successful execution of their strategy. They can't identify what is undermining and sabotaging their ability to get employees to align, to do what they need to do when they need to do it, and to achieve the mission of their organization. That lack of awareness of what's in the way is the biggest difference between the lowly ant and you and me.

Becoming Aware of the Execution Virus in Your Organization

In your workplace, as we've seen, there are hidden viral conversations that invade the thinking of your employees just as the fungus parasite infects the ant colony. And while the virus in your workplace won't kill you or your employees, it will have such a dramatic impact on your employees' behavior that it can obliterate your business, just as the ant parasite can wipe out an ant colony.

In Chapter 5, we talked about how memes may change as they encounter other ideas, resulting in new memes that may be more or less successful replicators than their predecessors. **This evolution of memes is the key to taking control of your business's future.**

Hidden conversations are a form of replicating memes, spreading throughout your organization by taking over your employees one by one. In a team or any group of people who interact together in a workplace, the wrong memes can become toxic and destructive to employee performance, undermining the execution of your strategy.

It may be difficult to understand how this information gets into our companies while we aren't looking—or why we remain unaware of such a powerful force. Regardless, memes will not be visible until you (*not* anybody else) expose them and you (*not* anybody else) reveal the truth about them and their impact on you and your employees' vision, awareness, connectedness, and accountability—the critical components of the complex evolving system that is your company.

The Execution Virus Will Never Die,
But There Is a Vaccine Against It—the Truth

Memes have a definite beginning, yet they have no end. Once a meme invades, it can never be eliminated. In fact, trying to eradicate memes, focusing on what you *don't* want, only fixes them more firmly (if surreptitiously) in your business.

Remember that memes—both positive and negative—can interact with other memes, creating new ones. So what vaccine can you give your organization to help it build a resistance to viral memes? The positive meme that acts as a vaccine against all the negative memes is *the truth.* Not just any truth, but the truth about your company's past performance and the exposure of any secrets, past and present. This truth needs to cover your most outrageous stories of success, your fabrications, your transgressions against and conduct toward others, and the business secrets that you think your employees don't know (although they most likely do).

Your past and the past of all the people you've brought into your organization are the source of viral memes. Imagine how much more effective your employees could be if you and they knew how memes work and how they have meticulously undermined all your best intentions to execute strategy.

It's Time to Get Vaccinated (and Then Get Regular
Booster Shots)

Though a negative, limiting meme can never be removed, it can be replaced with a positive meme through the following four-step process:

1. Tell the truth about your past—good and bad.

2. Identify the limiting and negative viral conversation—
   the meme—that represents your employees'
   interpretation of all past failures. Ask yourself and

your employees, "What do we say about ourselves and our company when we tell the truth about the failures we have experienced?"

3. Declare a positive future—a newly invented positive meme—to take the place of the negative viral meme. This is the truth of who you are, and it results in a powerful stand for the possibility of your shared future.

4. Adopt a system to keep the positive meme active and replicating throughout your organization. I use a promise-based execution management and feedback system to do just that, and it eventually replaces the negative, destructive meme in your language and thinking.

Throughout this process, you must remember that old memes never die; they just fade into the background to fight another day. That will happen as soon as you fall back into doing things the old way— through the exercise of power or force, for instance.

Because a meme is a language-based information gene that can replicate itself through thinking, speaking, and imitating behavior, the good news is that the technology for dealing with memes is available to all of us: language. Newly invented, positive counter-memes are the only effective ways of dealing with preexisting, destructive memes. Only through language can you declare and align as a group on a powerful counter-meme.

Unfortunately counter-memes have little or no staying power on their own. They are especially weak at first and need a new, conscious structure to support them and maintain their existence. If negative memes—and the automatic thinking patterns they engender among your team—have their roots in past failures, positive counter-memes are based on declared possibilities created through your words.

And here's the kicker: The memes your employees have? They probably caught them from you. As the leader, you are the most likely source of your organization's destructive thinking.

But you're undoubtedly not the only one. Plenty of carriers are capable of bringing subsequent memes into "the colony" and replicating them. In fact, every employee is infected, so every employee can be a host and a replicator, too. You need to vaccinate all of them, but you need to start with yourself. Only then can you begin building the structure to support the new meme that will immunize your organization. That structure takes the form of dialogue.

Dialogue Is the Antibody to the Execution Virus

Memes are one-sided conversations that people in your organization are having with themselves. Effectively, viral monologues like "It's their strategy," "They don't appreciate us," "They're always making excuses," or "they don't care" are conversations in which nobody's answering. The employees having these monologues are just repeating and replicating the meme that's been transmitted to them.

What negative monologues have you engaged in recently?

Are you committed to vaccinating yourself against the Execution Virus?

Dialogue acts as an antibody to negative viral memes. Authentic dialogue is truthful and transparent, so there is no opportunity for a hidden meme to take hold.

Begin by taking a hard look at yourself as a leader, which will help you rise to the challenge of transforming your company. How do you start? You need to ask yourself some very tough questions, and then you need to tackle another virus in your company. It's called the Entitlement Virus, and exposing and replacing that one is the first step toward exposing and replacing the Execution Virus. Once you've done both, you'll be well on your way to transforming your company and producing the breakthrough results you want.

Are You Leading or Just Pretending?

> "If you work hard
> enough and assert
> yourself, and use
> your mind and
> imagination, you
> can shape the world
> to your desires."
>
> Malcolm Gladwell

Real Leaders Are Responsible

Companies that reach for and attain true breakthrough performance are guided by leaders who understand what the company requires of them on a daily basis. It might sound trite to say that leadership is not a privilege but a responsibility; however, I truly believe that responsibility is the mainstay of authentic and effective leaders.

To illustrate what I'm talking about, here are ten characteristics of responsible leaders:

1. They acknowledge and fully appreciate the law of cause and effect. They believe nothing happens by chance.

2. They are 100 percent responsible for *whatever* happens, no matter what.

3. They do not hide behind reasons why results are not what they said they would be.

4. They transform the major issues in their lives by first transforming their relationship to circumstances. No matter how bad they think they have it, they don't try to avoid being responsible for their circumstances, since doing that would leave them powerless over what is happening in their lives.

5. They rarely utter the word "because." That's a word ineffective people hide behind, in an attempt to avoid responsibility. Put it in any sentence and you will see what I'm talking about: Everything after "because" is just cover.

6. They uncover the limiting paradigms they are allowing into their organizations and transform them into a stand for what's possible. In this way, they live responsibly with freedom and power.

7. They affirm their ultimate power to *say how* it's going be and then they make sure it is that way, acknowledging at the same time that ultimate power is the same as ultimate responsibility.

8. They hold themselves and others accountable by making sure everyone in the organization relates to each other according to their professional roles, or "accountabilities." Relating to others as their personal selves—treating someone as a friend, for example—undermines their capacity to be accountable and produce results.

9. They are aware of the conversations they engage in and are 100 percent responsible for them. They do not allow gossip or complaining to undermine integrity and create cynicism and apathy.

10. They take complete responsibility for the conversations that take place in their companies. *(This is the most important one!)*

Leaders are responsible for everything in their lives. It's a 100 percent proposition. It's all or nothing, and that's a tough place to stand. But there is no alternative if you want to be a genuinely powerful leader.

The Company Is Not About You, So Listen Up!

You cannot build an unstoppable company if the company is about you. You must remove yourself from the equation and take fundamental responsibility for the questions that get asked, because it's in the asking of questions that insight, innovation, and discovery happens.

It's a huge mistake to believe that your company will grow if you don't allow people around you to contribute to the overall direction of and growth within the company—even if you think you have all the answers. And you don't.

Your job is to build leaders, to be someone who lifts others up and gives them the responsibility to make mistakes and grow.

The company is about the organization you created to fulfill its mission, and it's about your employees (your internal clients) and your customers (your external clients).

The most important question a leader can ask is this: "What does this company truly need from me right now?" That is the primary focus of authentic leadership.

Real Leadership Versus the Pretense of Leadership

In the future, you will find that the management/leadership model you've always used, perhaps for decades, won't work in the new economy and the emerging workplace. If you want to lead your business out of the current calamities of the marketplace, you'll need to find a different way to look at who you are as a leader and who you are for your employees. Moreover, you'll need to determine who you *aren't.*

Ask yourself this fundamental question: "Am I truly committed to cultivating who I am as a *leader* for the future, or am I more interested in—and committed to—reinforcing the chronic *pretense of my leadership* and expecting everyone else to make the changes needed?"

That question may seem harsh or cynical, but most organizations today aren't going to survive the next five years unless their leaders realize that it's *their* thinking and *their* behavior that most stands in the way of their organization's success.

The predominant myth in business (and elsewhere) is that to be a leader whom people will follow, you must already "know" the answers or come with ready solutions to the most vexing problems your organization faces. If that's what you believe, then you're only pretending to lead. So on one hand there's leadership, and on the other there's the pretense of leadership. Which approach have you honestly adopted as your modus operandi?

Think of a time when you exercised authentic leadership— when you worked for your organization rather than making what happened about you. How did it feel? What were the results?

Think of a time when you carried on the pretense of leadership. How did it feel? What were the results?

Consequences of Pretending to Lead

Many leaders—even some very good leaders—struggle with and refuse to give up the *pretense* of leadership. More often than not, it's exactly this thinking and the behavior it produces that cause them to fail. This thinking covers up something that's missing. As a result, the entire company often gets diverted onto the wrong path, one that reflects the past.

The most obvious example of this is the way in which "leaders" in government and the financial industry created a subprime (or more accurately, substandard) mortgage industry that took down the economy of the United States and much of the rest of the world. People went merrily down the path of financial ruin, following leaders who would not allow others to contribute to the thinking that steered everyone into this mess. Greed certainly played a part. But it's impossible for greed to gain a foothold without the pretense of leadership that says, "I know best. Your way is wrong, and you need to follow us because only we can best take care of you." This kind of insidious paternalism makes an entire community weak.

The problem with allowing yourself to fall into a pretentious style of leadership is that you create a culture of patriarchy and paternalism. The message you send your employees is: "I own you (because I sign your paycheck), I know what's best for you (because I have the answers), and I will take care of you (because I have the best of intentions and want you to be loyal)."

In today's workplace, most employees and clients believe that is pure bullshit. They've lived through a financial disaster in which 600,000 people a week were added to unemployment lines. They wondered if they were next, and they've stopped trusting leadership—including yours. They've been told to hope that better times are coming, but as we discussed in Chapter 2, hope is as destructive as pretentious leadership. Hope has never been a winning strategy. It is a fictionalized version of reality, trafficked on so many levels and on so many street corners that it's become a commodity—and one that causes damage to those who believe in it.

You don't need to create more hope in your company. You need to open up a connection to and a conversation with your employees for things to happen that weren't going to happen otherwise.

Stop Pretending and Start Leading, Because Nobody's Buying Your B.S.

You might ask, "What if they figure it out? What if they realize that I don't possess all the insights, answers, and solutions to the challenges that face my organization? Then what?"

The answer is this: Then, you can start becoming a real leader.

The real problem in business is that most leaders aren't thinking about how to authentically improve their leadership. They're more concerned about making certain nobody knows that they don't have all the answers. They spend much of their time diligently covering up their poor decision making instead of working to build their business through others. Most leaders try hard to keep everyone in the dark about the fact that "they don't have it." But guess what? Nobody's buying it. Such behavior just makes employees return the favor. Most people who live in fear of losing the "deception of paternalism" aren't the CEOs. They're the employees who won't take responsibility for growing and expanding their roles. They'll simply continue to make their leader feel like the emperor while never daring to say that he or she has no clothes. That's the key point. Your employees already know you're just pretending, so continuing to pretend will do you no good. In fact, it'll just make things worse.

To Start Leading, Step Outside Your Comfort Zone

When you cling to the notion that you are only valued for your answers and that a leader without answers brings little value to his or her business, you teach your employees to think the same way. You create the next generation of pretending leaders.

Leadership is about stepping out of your comfort zone—getting out of the box—and the irony is that the instructions for getting out of the box are outside the box.

Begin by Stepping Out of the Past

Until you recognize that your true value as a leader is in your ability to *lead* an *inquiry* into the solutions for your organization (and not try to provide all the answers), you are doomed to repeat your own bad decisions and those of others who came before you. That's because the past has a grip on you that you can rarely see from your current perspective. It's there in the conversations you engage in, the choices you make, and the actions you take and direct others to take. You think that you can see what is ahead of you, and you think you know what you must do to avoid failure, but what you see as your future is really only a reflection of your past.

Until you uncover your old behavior as a leader and put that in the past where it belongs, all you can expect is incremental performance increases, if that. Breakthroughs are not born of past-based thinking.

Managers grasping for a way to fundamentally shift their organizations' performance have to recognize that most programs for change treat symptoms rather than the underlying conditions at the heart of the matter.

For example, when you reduce expenses to mitigate an impending drop in performance, you are merely addressing the symptoms. You have done nothing to alter the organization's thinking to operate more effectively. In fact, addressing symptoms is more damaging to your organization's performance because of the powerful and destructive memes created inside your organization.

A more powerful future is infinitely possible, but to own it, you must be willing to give up the pretense that as a leader, you always need to know the answers. Instead, you must begin to learn how to ask the right questions.

Are You Up to the Challenge of Becoming a Real Leader?

So, what are you going to choose for yourself from this point forward? If you're committed to seeing your company grow and prosper and become a real leader, then read on.

In the following months, your challenge will be to lead your team through a powerful inquiry that uncovers and reveals the true context of your organization. This conversation will permit you and all the stakeholders to renew your culture and discover possible results that up to now you've only dreamed of.

Reality Check:
Find Out If You're Leading or Just Pretending

To get a handle on whether you're really leading or just pretending to lead, read each of the monologues that come next. Each of them is a negative viral meme that infects leaders. Then score yourself on how closely that monologue matches your own thinking. Give yourself a score of 5 if your thinking matches the monologue or is very close to it and a 1 if the monologue does not match your thinking at all. Then add up your total score to see if you're leading or just pretending to lead. Once you know your total, read about the specific dangers of each of the ten ways of pretending to lead.

1. **Blaming your employees for not doing their job**

    "The market is bad and business is off. I need to find out which employees aren't pulling their weight so I can weed them out. They seemed so promising when I hired them, but they just haven't worked out. I've given them warnings, and they know that I've let others go before, so if they're going to survive, it's going to be pretty much up to them."

    Circle your score: 1   2   3   4   5

2. **Blaming the market**

    "My business is suffering, and something or someone is to blame. It's the market, or the president, or Congress, or the bank. All I have time for is putting out fires and solving huge breakdowns. Nothing's working, yet I'm doing all I can just to keep up—and I resent it."

    Circle your score: 1   2   3   4   5

3. Changing your strategy

"Everyone has some kind of strategy, and I've spent a lot of time perfecting mine. When my business isn't growing, I go back to perfect the plan or redo it."

Circle your score: 1   2   3   4   5

4. Failing to embrace chaos

"It's chaotic enough around here with all the problems we have getting the work out the door and serving clients. I'm trying to get rid of the chaos, so we can get some work done. I spend lots of time putting out fires, and I wish I could just get time to work through some issues and find solutions that everyone can work with. But I don't have the time. It's too crazy around here."

Circle your score: 1   2   3   4   5

5. Addressing symptoms instead of core issues

"When there's a breakdown that causes us to miss a deadline or fail to deliver on a promise to a client, the first thing I must do is determine if it is a problem that needs fixing, and then go to work to get the problem solved. Often, that involves figuring out who is at fault and establishing new rules to prevent it from happening again."

Circle your score: 1   2   3   4   5

6. Deviating from your core business

"When there is a limit on how I can expand and find new vertical markets, I begin to dream about what else I can provide my clients so they won't leave. I'm looking for something that'll really undermine my competition."

Circle your score: 1   2   3   4   5

7. Being attached to outcomes

"If I'm not sure of the outcome, its best to avoid the risk, so I don't end up failing and then having to deal with the aftermath. If something goes wrong, then there's something very wrong with me and my abilities."

Circle your score: 1   2   3   4   5

8. Managing people rather than promises and failing to value employee promises as you would any other valuable asset in your company

"It's tough to ask people to put their ass on the line for something important for the growth and profitability of my company. Hell, it's tough to put my own ass on the line. If I told people that I was taking an important action, they'd hold me accountable for following through. That's really scary, so I won't hold them accountable for their promises if they'll let me off the hook for mine. After all, I need to treat my employees with respect, and when things don't get done, it's often for a very good reason. If I told them they absolutely need to keep their word or don't bother coming to the next meeting, they'd resent me, and all the other employees would think I was bullying them into working harder. I'd probably lose some pretty good employees, and I can't afford to have that happen."

Circle your score: 1   2   3   4   5

9. Failing to pay attention to the conversations you lead

"I've been in business for years, I know what it takes to be successful, and I know what my employees need to do to make "our" projections. They just need to do it the way I did it, and they need to listen to me about how to do it. I don't have time to sit down and go back and forth with people about what they think should be different or changed. I pay them all well, and I just want to see the performance out of them that reflects their paychecks."

Circle your score: 1   2   3   4   5

10. Treating your employees like family

"This company is my baby. I started this company with just me, and I want everyone to get along. Today there are 100 of us, and it's important I take care of my business—and them—you know, like I did with my own kids."

Circle your score: 1   2   3   4   5

Rating Your Results

Score   Results

1-15   Congratulations, you've passed the reality check! You haven't fallen victim to the ten main ways of pretending to be a leader. To drive home the point about how crucial it is to continue leading and not pretending, read on about the dangers of the ten ways of pretending to lead.

16-30   You've got one foot in reality. You're probably doing an okay job of leading some of the time, but you're falling victim to comforting thought patterns you've learned from others, and they're causing you to *pretend* that you're leading some-times as well. You need to step out of your comfort zone so you can get back to reality and start becoming a real leader 100 percent of the time.

31-50   Oh yes, you're the Great Pretender. You've created or inherited a business culture that rewards the pretense of leadership rather than real leadership.

As a result, your company is disconnected and not executing your strategy. Read on to find out the ten things you're doing to yourself and your company by just pretending to lead. Then make a commitment to stop pretending and start the process of becoming a real leader.

The Consequences of the Ten Ways of Just Pretending to Lead

1. **Blaming your employees**

Sure, there will be employees who simply can't cut it, and it may be better for you if they were not cutting it somewhere else. But if your employees watch you dismiss people who in the past were doing great and today are struggling, that creates the negative viral meme of "The boss is watching, so just don't screw up." Smart and talented employees struggle at times, and that's a fact you need to accept. Beyond that, committed yet struggling employees are usually a symptom of a much deeper problem that you can't see and haven't yet addressed.

2. **Blaming the market**

It's easier to look out there and blame everyone else than to look within and see that for years, you've stuck with the same strategy, the same products, and the same solutions that made you successful in the beginning. If you've been in business for even three years, the world has changed during that time. There have been major paradigm shifts, and while you were busy working *in* your business; you forgot to work *on* your business. Futurist Joel Arthur Barker has said, "When the paradigm shifts, everyone goes back to zero."[12] Some people shift to respond to the new paradigm; others never see change coming.

3. Changing your strategy

When business volume falls off, the first thing many leaders do is convene a new strategy session. But reacting with a new strategy—a new or different list of things to do—could be the worst thing possible. While 87 percent or more of companies don't ever fully achieve their strategy, it's usually not the strategy that's the problem. The reason most people do strategic planning is to have a road map to remind them where they said they were headed, but most written strategies end up on shelves or in drawers.

A good strategy is actually a conversation for the future of your organization. If you're a $10 million company and you want to be a $20 million company, the conversations you engage in need to change. A strategic plan is not a goal to get to—it's a conversation that calls you to *be* (a $20 million company, for example) in the future. It's insufficient and foolish to scale your strategy to fit the next level of growth. You need an entirely new conversation for the company you want to build. If you want to be a $50 million company, start thinking and talking like one. Imagine what that company will look like when you get there. Then stand in your imagined future and begin to describe how you got there.

4. Failing to embrace chaos

Chaos is a dirty word in most people's vocabulary, but when you think of chaos you're probably thinking of tumult. Merriam-Webster defines *chaos* variously as

> "the confused unorganized state of primordial matter before the creation of distinct forms" or "the inherent unpredictability in the behavior of a complex natural system."

Chaos is natural and unavoidable, and it gives rise to the new. In business, chaos is transformative; it creates urgency and is represented by a creative tension that causes people to excel. Merriam-Webster defines *tumult* as

> "a disorderly agitation or milling about of a crowd, usually with uproar and confusion of voices; a turbulent uprising; a violent outburst."

Tumult does not lead to creativity. It just stresses people out and drives down performance. So don't fear chaos. In the end, allowing it to happen can be one of the most powerful aspects of your strategy.

5. Addressing symptoms instead of core issues

It's only natural when disruptive issues pop up in the workplace that the first thing we want to do is snuff them out as fast as we can. That rarely works. Most of the time, it just temporarily masks the real problem, which continues to have a detrimental impact on workplace performance.

Disruption is a symptom of other issues. Perhaps you can't see it now because when the pressure is off, it feels like you nipped it in the bud. But you didn't; you just addressed the symptoms. The core issues remain, so they will just show up somewhere else, and you will go through the same exercise of pulling people in and talking through the problem (actually symptoms) again and again and again.

6. Deviating from your core business.

When you are suffering sales losses due to the recession or because the competition is beating you at your own game, it may seem logical to seek a new vertical market, change markets, or even add to your core products and services. That's usually a horrible mistake! Stick to your core, because plenty of businesses don't and thereby create disasters for themselves.

For example, a client of mine was finding it difficult to compete because other companies were encroaching on their niche market. Without any research, my client decided that the best way forward was to start a new online business that was somewhat related to its core business; it would serve the same client base. Management thought their core clientele would go for the new concept and would thus spend more money, but the strategy was a complete disaster.

The company spent $20 million setting up this business, and not one client was interested—not one. To say leadership didn't do their homework would be an understatement. In addition to bypassing the marketing legwork to understand their clients' needs, they got wrapped up in the excitement of having a new idea, and the new endeavor sapped critical energy from their core business. The new $20 million business bit the dust within a year.

7. Being attached to outcomes

You've heard it before: "What you resist persists." Time and time again, I've seen people focus on the negative aspect of something—and what they get is more negative results. If you are attached to not failing, it makes failing more vivid from your perspective. All you see are threats of failure. When you're working hard not to fail, you can't be working on winning at the same time. You need to stay focused on what you desire as on outcome rather than focusing on what you want to avoid or what you don't want.

You have zero control over the circumstances in your life, and the faster you figure that out, the happier and more successful you'll be. Trying to change your circumstances can consume all your time and energy. So let go. Be the best you can be and never get attached to hoped-for outcomes.

When you create a plan, don't get attached to it. If you fail at it, you're not a failure. Failure is not the end of the world; it's a milestone in your education. You've heard the quote "Fail fast and fail often." Well, get to it. It's part of upgrading the conversations in your life from the ones you had as a child—about how fear of failure is a good thing—to an adult conversation about how failure is what happened yesterday. Today is an opportunity to create a new possibility.

8. **Managing people rather than promises and failing to value employee promises**
At one time or another most of us make promises to ourselves and others. But do we really value them? To build a THIRTEENER company or to just bring in the next great client requires a new level of rigor in making and keeping promises. It requires a new relationship to your own promises and to the promises other people make to you. Simply put, you have to deliver on your own promises and hold others to doing the same. You probably don't do the latter very often; you may simply hope others will have the integrity to do what they say they will. And then, when they don't deliver, you allow yourself to completely buy into the other person's reasons why. As a result, 87 percent of strategies don't get executed.

So stop trying to manage people. Start managing promises, and see things begin to move.

9. **Failing to pay attention to the conversations you lead**
After ten years of study, I've discovered that Best Place to Work companies value entirely different internal

conversations from the conversations valued by non-Best Place companies. What are the crucial conversations? According to employee reports, it's the conversations that show that their leaders consider them important.

Employees want to be acknowledged for their value, so the *quality* of the conversations and the *quantity* of these *quality* conversations will ultimately determine whether your organization will be a Best Place to Work. If that is not so important to you, consider that Best Place to Work companies deliver 2.5 to 3 times *more value* to the bottom line and to their owners than do others. Is that important to you?

10. Treating your employees like family

This is one of the biggest mistakes you can make. It's so big, in fact, that I devote the entire next chapter to its main consequence: entitlement. I hear many "proud papas" (and mamas) talk about their company's family atmosphere, but I shake my head in amazement at how limiting that thinking really is. Treating your employees like a family promotes patriarchy in your organization, and that saps all sense of urgency from your team by teaching that they can't think or act without first checking with "Daddy" or "Mommy." It limits an organization's ability to grow and feeds the narcissistic proclivities of entrepreneurial CEOs. And it does one more thing: It creates entitlement, which is a virus that's most noticeable in companies where leadership seems to be giving everything they can think of to keep their employees satisfied so they will remain with the company.

Once they've caught the Entitlement Virus, employees demand more and more from the employment relationship, and they often actually withhold their commitment and performance if they don't get what they want. They do that for one simple reason: It's not their company. It's Daddy's or Mommy's.

That's the last thing you want if you're trying to create a THIRTEENER company. My advice: Get your maternal and paternal needs met at home. The more you treat people like they need to depend on you, the more they will avoid an important move until you say so. That means you'll have to be there at every turn, and it also means that no one will grow. Not them. Not you.

"Employees have three prime needs: Interesting work, recognition for doing a good job, and being let in on things that are going on in the company"

– Zig Ziglar

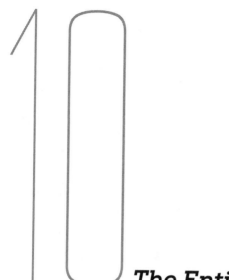

The Entitlement Virus

> *"Entitlement and privilege corrupt."*
>
> Vice Admiral James B. Stockdale

In addition to the Execution Virus, which undermines the performance of so many companies, you need to be aware of the Entitlement Virus if you expect to lead a THIRTEENER organization. Even the very best companies I know have the Entitlement Virus, and your company probably has been infected with it as well.

Entitlement Infection

One quiet Saturday afternoon, I was sitting in my office at the far end of what I assumed was an empty building. As I was working, I heard the printer down the hall spitting out documents. I hadn't hit the print button on my computer, so I took a look around. Only one office had its lights on. I moseyed over to where the printed documents were to see what was going on. It turned out that one of my employees was about to resign and start his own company. He was planning to compete against us, and he was making copies of our proprietary business documents. Apparently, he thought he was entitled to take what he wanted. Had I not been there, this employee's feeling of entitlement would have resulted in our confidential information being taken.

This is not to say that employees who feel entitled are going to steal intellectual property or even that all employees are infected with the Entitlement Virus. But some will feel they are entitled to help themselves to things they want, and the sad fact is that 95 percent of all companies experience employee theft. It may be as small as employees taking home office supplies, or it could be as serious as millions of dollars embezzled by a trusted bookkeeper.

A sense of entitlement prevents you, your employees, and your company from meeting the challenges of competition and growth. In his transformational 1993 book *Stewardship: Choosing Service over Self-Interest*, Peter Block stated, "At the heart of entitlement is the belief that my needs are more important than the business and that the business exists for my sake."[13] I've dealt with this issue myself, when a downturn in business made me want to keep my employees at any cost. I discovered that the need to nurture familial-type relationships with employees was a double-edged sword.

When I related to my employees as if they were members of my extended family, I made it nearly impossible to hold them accountable. That created a bad precedent for getting important work done in the future—not with my longtime employees, but with others who had joined later and realized this was a place where you didn't really have to work very hard, be on time, do what's promised, or even complete assigned duties with any degree of enthusiasm or integrity.

The Entitlement Virus impacts performance by infecting the thinking of employees and leaders alike, and it works symbiotically with the Execution Virus, each one keeping the other in place. And as with other viral memes, you can't see the Entitlement Virus. You can only see its symptoms, so remember this: When you are trying your best to solve a problem and nothing is working, consider that the real problem is invisible to you. It's under the surface, and you're going to need to ask different questions to get to its source.

Like with the Execution Virus, you can neutralize the negative Entitlement Virus by replacing it with a positive virus: Empowerment.

What Is Entitlement, and Where Does It Come From?

Anyone who has ever owned or managed a business has experienced the impact of entitlement and wondered what to do about it. It's a covert issue that drives most CEOs crazy. As I've said, entitlement is most noticeable when leaders appear to be doing everything they can possibly think of to keep their employees satisfied and with the company, while those same employees demand more from the employment relationship and then withhold their commitment and performance if they don't get it.

Entitlement is a real problem that will prevent you from executing your strategy, but it's merely the symptom of more dangerous underlying conditions. Employees who think they are entitled often feel as though they are victims of management exploitation or mistreatment. Left unchecked, entitlement can result in covert acts of revenge. Therefore, it's important to understand what's at the source of your employees' entitlement thinking. Your company's future depends on it.

Patriarchy Is at the Root

I believe that the root cause of the Entitlement Virus an be attributed to two issues:

1) The fear of losing, which makes clients, employees, and others more important than the business;

2) A pretense of leadership that claims employees are more important than management, although, in fact, management believes chiefly in its own entitlement.

Entitlement is the result of a patriarchal belief system that most of us share—a belief system often designed around financial control and the idea that you must maintain a clear line of authority to operate your business: Entitlement implies that if you're the boss, you are endowed with special privileges that others don't have, and it arises when management wants to avoid being seen by employees as taking advantage of the system for their own gain.

To believe in entitlement as a leader, you must first operate under the arrogant assumption that you're making all the sacrifices and that, therefore, you should be entitled to something extra. After all, it's your company. At the same time, you are trying to hide that you're doing well; you might even become indignant if someone suggested that you were making all the money and not paying others what they "deserve." Finally, you're telling yourself that if employees knew how much you were "raking in" compared to what you pay them, they just might up and leave. All this lets you extend the fiction that no such issue exists. And that will come back to bite you, because you're only fooling yourself.

In reality, you *are* entitled to something special. You ought to be making significantly more money than your highest-ranking employee. Why are you trying to justify your salary to yourself? When you have a good year, do you jack up everyone's salary? No, you don't do anything of the kind. Instead, you find a way to give people a nice reward along with verbally demonstrated appreciation. And that's exactly what you should do, not go off half-cocked out of guilt, trying to make up to others for your good fortune. That's just another pretense of leadership, and it's the pretending that is hurting you.

Even if employees come and tell you that they think they should get a raise, having your best year in business doesn't mean you have to start overpaying employees. Once you overcompensate by raising a salary, you can *never* bring it back down without consequences.

Have you ever felt owed by your business for the effort you put in?

Have you ever felt guilty about your employees' compensation, even while knowing they are paid fairly?

Who Has the Entitlement Virus, and What Does It Do to Them?

So to paraphrase Peter Block, the viral meme that best encapsulates the Entitlement Virus is "The employees' needs are more important than the business." As for who has been infected by this meme, the answer is managers who are trying to prevent employees from withholding their efforts unless they receive extra perks. Employees will know when you're trying not to lose business, not lose good employees, not lose your best clients, or not lose face.

Managers who are infected by the Entitlement Virus think they're doing what's best for the company by overlooking infractions such as coming in late or taking longer lunch periods. These are the things that my clients complain most about. It drives them crazy. What's the big deal with a little tardiness, they ask themselves, or missing a client's deadline, or helping yourself to a pencil or a pad of paper for your kid's homework?

The answer is the loss of integrity. Little infractions turn into huge issues over time. But the real cost of ignoring this kind of thing is that it keeps your organization from operating with integrity. It's an infected strategy that derails attempts at resolving even the slightest conflicts between you and your employees.

When managers believe their own sacrifices entitle them to special benefits, that belief creates feelings of entitlement among the rank and file as well. Management is the primary source of entitlement thinking, and therefore, only management can transform the negative Entitlement Virus into the positive Empowerment Virus.

The Plan of Attack

To attack the virus of entitlement, take these five steps:

1. **First, eliminate the ridiculous conversation that begins, "We're like family around here."**
   If I had $10 for every time a CEO told me he or she tried to treat employees like family, I'd be on a yacht in the Caribbean. Sure, it sounds good when you say it, and it might seem like it's desirable to create close relationships because they purportedly feel good to everyone. But the

fact remains that most families are dysfunctional. Why would you want that kind of dysfunctional behavior in your company, too?

All families tend to be patriarchal or matriarchal by nature. So even with the best of intentions, trying to create a business culture that's like a family ends up ultimately breeding sibling rivalry, jealousies, and resentments. And as in your family (and in mine, too), accountability is usually absent most of the time. When employees become familiar with each other, they tend to stop holding each other accountable because nobody wants to step on friends' or siblings' toes.

Start relating to employees according to their account-ability (that is, in the job they hold or the professional role they play) instead of their personality (their privileged position in the company). The "vice president of marketing" is an accountability; my Starbucks buddy Anastas isn't.

The big shift usually takes place when you ask employees to make real promises to take real actions and then measure how well they have kept their promises. If they don't do the job, rather than getting upset, simply be curious. Ask, "What's missing that kept you from keeping your word?" Then, begin working with the employee to close the gap by helping to provide what's missing. Doing this one thing will cause immense change within your company.

2. **Next create a structure for fulfilling promises.**
    When employees know what your vision for your company is and how they contribute to its fulfillment, they can make meaningful promises to accomplish things that will make a difference to the bottom line. But that requires a different kind of conversation from you as their leader.

The first thing you need to do is knock off all the talk about all your great ideas. Sure, you're an entrepreneur; you're going to have great ideas. But you don't have to blab about them out loud, so stop talking about all the things "we're going to do" in the future. Focus on your core business issues and start promising the specific measurable actions *you* are going to take right now. Rather than talking to your employees about what you will do in the future, *be* an example right now of what you want from your employees.

Managers literally stop the action when they confuse "talking *about* taking action" with actually taking action. They collapse the two into each other. For example, you may hold a meeting to talk about how to solve a problem or how you're going to get a desirable new client, but a week later, you have the same problem because no action has been taken. No one is managing and measuring the promises for taking action; they're simply managing "talking about" taking action. So get into action and hold employees accountable, and then start measuring for what you want. Those are the only things that matter.

3. **Communicate fully.**

   If you are keeping secrets of any kind in your company, you are building resentment, and feelings of entitlement will emerge, if they haven't already. Without information, employees cannot be expected to act in ways that support your vision. Instead, they begin to make things up, and what they make up is either not the truth or wrong 99 percent of the time. Do you want that going on in your company?

   When you withhold information, you teach your people that withholding is a value. Most likely it's not a value you want. Not fully communicating means you don't trust anyone with important information. And if you don't trust your employees, your employees won't trust you.

4. **Understand that alignment is a leader's work of art.**
Years ago, a great coach, Mitzie Hoelscher, taught me that alignment was my principal job as a leader. Nothing moves in an organization unless there is alignment with the vision and mission. Without it, there is no accountability, and in turn, no accountability means no alignment. They go hand in hand. You won't mitigate entitlement if you're not aligned, and you can't align if you're not accountable.

5. **Finally, make sure all employees understand that if you can't count on them to do what they said they'd do, you don't need them.**
We hold on to some employees longer than we should. There's no reason to keep employees who have no intention of keeping their word. But if employees aren't keeping their word, the first place we need to look is at our relationship to our own word. If what we say and what we do don't match, people begin to believe it's not important for them to keep their word, either.

You'll know you have a problem in this area when you notice employees breaking agreements with clients.

When we think we don't have to keep our word because of our position or rank, we breed the Entitlement Virus, which spreads rapidly and is hard to knock out, even with our best strategies. An entitlement mentality exists, to one degree or another, in every organization. To neutralize it requires that people be put in charge of themselves and be allowed to choose how they will perform. With those privileges come responsibility, accountability, and a purposeful alignment with the vision and mission. However, that presumes that the purpose is well communicated and well understood.

Replacing the Entitlement Virus with the Empowerment Virus

When employees are put in charge of themselves, are told clearly what the purpose of the company is and their purpose within the company, when they are allowed to choose how they will perform, and are told that they and their leaders will be held accountable for their actions, they become empowered. They are responsible for their own future.

That creates an Empowerment Virus that employees can transmit and replicate among themselves and that serves as the best counteragent to the Entitlement Virus. Those who won't commit to empowerment and accountability tend to self-select out when it's clear they aren't on the same path as everyone else.

As a leader, your only choices are to take responsibility for performance *and* continue to enjoy the benefits of behaving like a conscious leader—or not. Choosing not to perform as promised means you'll have to accept the consequences of your actions. The Entitlement Virus has the power to prevent any organization from reaching its objectives. When you as the leader can grasp the notion that it begins with you and you are squarely at the source of this issue, you can examine your own conversations around entitlement.

To summarize, when managers believe their own sacrifices entitle them to the special benefits of a privileged class, the Entitlement Virus, and feelings of entitlement will show up among the employees. Only by creating awareness of the Entitlement Virus will you be in a position to transform it into the positive Empowerment Virus.

Key Points and Preparing for What's Next

Before we get into the process of how to transform your company into a THIRTEENER company, let's review what we've covered in Sections 1 and 2:

1. **Business is a network of consciously connecting or unconsciously disconnecting conversations.**
   Some conversations support conscious connection, a state of being in which employees feel that they belong and can contribute to the company's success and in which the power of the Breakthrough Strategy can flow throughout the organization and be executed. Other conversations create unconscious disconnection, a state of being in which many employees feel disempowered and in which employees struggle and often fail to execute the organization's strategy. Transforming your business into a consciously connected company requires transforming the conversations that constitute your business. If you can transform those conversations, then you'll get to *say how* your future will be.

2. **There are ten positive, consciously connecting conversations that produce connectedness within an organization.**
   I call these the ConnectionPoints™, and they help you powerfully and consciously lead an organization using the conversations for contribution, acknowledgment and appreciation, alignment, accountability, communication, relatedness, responsibility, integrity, possibility, and fun.

3. **There are many types of negative, disconnecting conversations that create disconnected companies.**
   These mostly take the form of viral memes, which show up in the form of hidden monologues that employees transmit

between themselves to create the "genetic code" of your organization. One type of negative viral meme is what I call an Execution Virus. Examples include "It's their strategy (not ours)," "They're always making excuses," "We've always done it this way," and "The boss is watching, so just don't screw up." Another kind of negative viral meme is the Entitlement Virus. This virus, which mainly infects management, is best encapsulated in the meme, "The employees' needs are more important than the business."

4. **Once a viral meme is in your company (and remember, all companies have memes), you can't overpower it, but you can replace it with a positive viral meme that you generate.**
   To do so you need to:

   a. Tell the truth about past transgressions, behavior, and results.

   b. Declare an affirmative future in the form of a positive meme that will take the place of the negative meme.

   c. Adopt a promise-based execution management and feedback system to keep the positive meme in existence, alive, and reinforced within your organization.

   d. Institute transparent dialogue with and between your employees to prevent new negative viral memes from forming.

Here Be Dragons

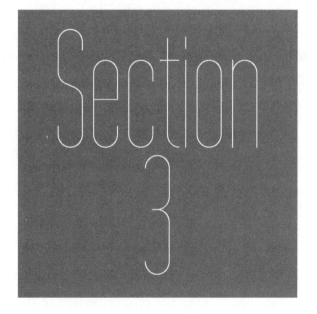

Section 3

Here Be Dragons: Real and Imagined Dangers

In the chapters ahead you'll find new insights for your leadership, new ways to think that will prepare you to take your organization into a previously undreamed of future.

What your company desperately needs to succeed is for you to take responsibility for providing authentic leadership, not the pretense of leadership. That means uncovering what's available to you that your employees and others possess and can express in ways that you never thought of.

As an authentic leader, you must be willing to not always play it safe. In fact, you must be willing to be vulnerable and open to recognize your own fears and weaknesses. And that's the first thing we're going to tackle in Section 3, starting with the process of authentic leadership.

11

Stepping Out of Your Comfort Zone

"You're off the edge of
the map now, mate.
And here be dragons!"

Captain Jack Sparrow in
Pirates of the Caribbean

Risking What You Have . . . To Have What You Want

Leadership is about stepping out of your comfort zone, and the instructions for getting out of your comfort zone are themselves outside your comfort zone. I've begun the process by making you ask yourself some tough questions about whether you're leading or just pretending to lead and also by showing you how pretending to lead is creating the Entitlement Virus in your company. Now it's time to take the second step: getting both feet out of your comfort zone and into the unknown.

I know that's a scary thought. As the iconic horror writer H. P. Lovecraft said, "The oldest and strongest emotion of mankind is fear, and the oldest and strongest kind of fear is fear of the unknown."[14] But fear is what's holding you back, and only by facing that fear and mastering it will you be able to get your company out of its proverbial rut and take it where you want it to go.

Terra Incognita: Exploring Unknown Territory

It's said that cartographers once labeled unexplored or unknown territory on their maps with the phrase "Here be dragons." The idea was to denote allegedly dangerous places, where sea serpents and other mythological creatures might lurk. Myths like this have always played a part in our lives, and that includes business.

As we've discovered, your business is made up of the thinking and conversations that go on undetected yet have great power over results, and the primary—and most destructive—meme that operates in the background is fear. Fear is the source of the Execution Virus and a mind-set that stifles individuals and groups. Those who are infected fear looking bad to others or being negatively judged or assessed. That prevents your organization from executing your strategy.

Fears like these originate in the kind of *prelogical* thinking that's common to preteens who are beginning to break away from parents or primary caretakers and are coping with the feeling of not belonging.

That doesn't necessarily mean that organizations are staffed by employees who think like preteens, but under stress and confronted by something that disrupts their feeling of belonging, employees often revert to preteen reactions. They may behave in ways that might appear childish.

Prelogical thinking often concerns myths, legends, limiting beliefs, and fears—all kinds of stuff that humans make up. However, prelogical thinking is not a very useful tool in the workplace, and employees who think this way are very difficult to motivate.

We all have a tendency to reject anything new and instead to stay with what is known or comfortable. This is how prelogical thinking hinders our ability to use rational thought to solve a problem. Our emotional ties to the past prevent us from seeing the real problem and push us to merely address the symptoms.

As I've said before, 87 percent of all companies with a strategic plan will fail to execute it. That's because those companies are pursuing the simplest yet most damaging strategy: *the strategy to avoid failure.*

You might ask, "Are you saying my strategy causes failure because I'm focused on making sure I don't fail?" Yes, that's exactly what I'm saying! Most people are invested in not failing, and they've taught all their employees to value that course of over taking any kind of risks that have the potential to pay off. Everyone's doing it, and it's costing them on a grand scale.

> **What kinds of failure make you most anxious?**
>
> **How do you work to avoid failure?**

I believe the leading causes of failure to execute business strategy are: (a) the unwillingness of business leaders and their followers to change their thinking from "avoiding failure" to "standing for something that seems to be impossible to achieve" and (b) the invention of conversations that support that avoidance-of-failure thinking.

In teaching others to let go of their fears about what might happen if they take risks, I've seen miracles happen. A professional services firm had an unprecedented 60 percent leap in performance in five months, for example. A creative services group went from a loss of tens of thousands of dollars in one year to a place on the *Inc.* 500/5,000 list and a more than 40,000 percent increase in net profit during the following years.

How Is That Possible? What Changed?

No one was fired. A few people left on their own when they decided they didn't want to let go of their accustomed ways of working. But nothing was altered in the businesses' overall strategies. All that changed was the willingness to let go of, past-based thinking. In a few short months, three things happened:

1. The leaders discovered the viral thinking that was preventing them and their employees from keeping promises and executing strategy.

2. All employees, including the leaders, changed their personal perspective of the core business.

3. All employees altered their relationship to the circumstances that had always left them feeling fear about failing, loss, or scarcity.

When management learned that their thinking was getting in their way, they were able to invent a new place to stand and lead from. That's the magic of understanding and uncovering the Execution Virus. When you uncover the specific viral meme that plagues your organization and then expose it to the light of day, the meme loses its power to drive your organization in the wrong direction, and you recover your power to have what you really want.

It sounds simple, and it is—unless you are unwilling to give up the past that runs you, your employees, and your business. Sometimes you have to be willing to get off the map before you can see where you've been on it.

Rowers and Growers

Over time, I have observed that all business strategies fall into two basic categories:

1. **Rower Strategy**: Operating from the past or reacting in ways that are based on fear of failure. I call this the Rower Strategy, because it reminds me of someone who's working hard but getting nowhere fast because he's rowing upstream, trying to get away from the dangerous rapids downstream. And he's all by himself in the boat. I know a lot of people who operate like this—and they're failing.

2. **Grower Strategy**: Focusing on building and generating from a perspective of the future—a view that is declared by *saying how* it's going to be. I call this the Grower Strategy.

Whenever I work with an organization, once I hear the conversations that are running their strategy, I can tell whether I'm dealing with a dysfunctional organization that's rooted in the past (the Rower Strategy) or a focused and functional organization that is building from a perspective of the future (a Grower Strategy). Believe me, there are more of the first than the second.

It's impossible to use both strategies at the same time, though infrequently an organization can move back and forth between the two. But the Rower Strategy usually prevails, because the past has a more powerful grip on people and their behavior than does the future, which has to be invented into existence.

The first sign of a Rower Strategy is management's attitude toward an outsider being brought into the company to work with them. The first reaction is, "Oh, gawd, here we go again. Now what are we going to do?"

If you want breakthrough results, you will need to move your organization away from "Here we go again" thoughts and into a place where people connect with each other and to the vision and mission of the company. That's a Grower Strategy, and that's where you will come into your own as a leader. But you don't just move your organization there; you must move yourself there first!

You must venture into unknown territory. You have to embrace your own fears, the myths you have made up, and whatever you're resisting before you can truly lead others. Otherwise your employees will see right through your pretense.

Some of my clients have tried to bring change to their employees so they wouldn't have to confront the dragons of their own past, but as they found out when employees resigned, that rarely works very well. However, once you follow a Grower Strategy, you can do just about anything because you won't have Rower Strategy results.

Don't Look Back. You Don't Know What's Ahead, So Say How It Will Be!

In a Grower Strategy, you enter the world of the unknown. The moment you look back for some kind of certainty that you are on the right path, you're right back in a Rower Strategy. But it's the adventure and not the destination that we are working toward here. You don't know—and you don't know what you don't know—that awaits you. You have to discover it.

Grower Strategy is about inventing something from nothing. That means if you think you already have the answer to your strategy execution issues, you are stuck in Rower Strategy, and the Execution

Virus is determining your future. Instead you need to be investigating what's possible at all times. Grower Strategy is not about your knowing the answers—it's about discovering the future you want. It's the quest for something worth pursuing, where you and your team can declare it to be and then have it be that way.

Why approach it this way? Because, either way, it's all made up. You can make it up to escalate results (Grower Strategy), or you can hang on to what you've made up that brings performance down (Rower Strategy).

Why not generate a radical and revolutionary innovation for a future that does not represent your fears of repeating the past? You let go of how you think it has to be and trust the process, allowing others to contribute innovative ideas and get connected to your vision. You'll never know how talented your employees are if you think you have to have all the answers.

Letting Go

In 2001, after I sold my software business to a competitor, I agreed to stay on, but I also had to confront the truth that my heart really wasn't in it. I knew that it was going to be "their way or the highway" so ultimately I headed on down the highway.

To do that, I had to let go of my view that I, as the former CEO, was bringing a solution to the new company's problems, that they needed my valuable insight to succeed, and that I even knew what was needed and wanted in the newly merged company.

It wasn't my business any longer; I had only a partial stake. I had to face the reality that they really wanted to do it their way, without my input. Confronting my own arrogance was painful, but the end result was a personal breakthrough: I took myself out of the equation, and I found my freedom.

I discovered that it's only when you are finally willing to risk all that you have—to let it all go, forfeit it—that you can actually have it. It's only then that you can invent a new future for yourself.

The past has your future in its grip, and when you have no awareness of the strength of that grip, you have few choices available. You are bound to the past, and the past owns your future.

I've been there, too, and much of the rest of this book is about why it doesn't have to be that way for you and what you can do about it. Section 4 deals with that transformative process, but you can't begin until you make an unconventional shift in your perspective—in the way you relate to circumstances of the past and the notion of a future-based organization.

12

Chaos:
The Great Transformer

> "Then you will
> know the truth,
> and the truth shall
> set you free."
>
> John 8:32

> "When John wrote
> that bit of good
> news, he forgot
> one important part:
> Before it does,
> it's going to kick
> your ass!"
>
> Daniel F. Prosser

The Failure to Embrace Chaos

As I've discovered for myself, the fundamental reason why so many leaders don't lead their teams to the finish line in executing their strategy is that they can't tolerate the discomfort that comes with the chaos when things aren't happening as planned.

Staying the course in the face of disorder, disequilibrium, or confusion is difficult. Most people can't do it. This is where the Rower Strategy—the avoidance of failure—plays a big part. Chaos is not an issue most organizations are keen to address; it's easier to address the crisis of the moment than to address the feeling of disequilibrium that comes along with the feeling of chaos. Instead of just accepting that a feeling of disequilibrium is natural in chaotic situations, most leaders want to look for a way to create the pretense of balance.

Rather than staying the course and waiting for the source of the breakdown to reveal itself, the CEO feels he or she needs to act, to do something to overcome the sense of being out of control—reacting to unpleasant events, for example, or blaming someone else for not doing the right thing, Above all, this leader wants to overcome the feeling of loss or avoid a possible failure.

I've done that myself, and all the clients I've worked with over the past ten years, from solo entrepreneurs to multimillion-dollar CEOs, have shared with me that they experience this helpless, out-of-control feeling when they are confronted by threats to their established plans. Panic sets in due to a drop in quarterly earnings, bad news from a major client, or the disappointment of a promising deal falling through.

It's undoubtedly happened to you, too. Perhaps one of your most important clients informed you he or she was considering a switch to a competitor. In that case, you might have to lay people off. Sure you could have done something a long time ago to prevent this from happening, but now you have to deal with something you didn't anticipate.

When you experience the anxiety that you're not equal to the challenge at hand, you're in the middle of a chaotic episode. Adrenaline courses through your veins, blood seems to rush out of your face. The shock of the situation makes it feel necessary to do something right now. Making a change and addressing the situation may make you feel better, but it only deals with the symptom and not with the real cause of the situation.

The Danger of the Urge to "Just Do Something"

The biggest mistake I've seen business leaders make in chaotic situations is rushing to judgment. They try to make sense of the situation and then immediately react. I say, "react," not "act," because to act would mean being "at cause," being in control of their life after considering the situation and allowing the sense of chaos to settle.

Unfortunately, the first decisions made in incidents like this tend to be the worst decisions. They are the ones leaders have to make amends for later.

Here's an example: I was sitting with the CEO of a well-established health-care firm. He had just learned that one of the maintenance workers had been seen painting a building for someone else during business hours. As I heard him talk about the incident on the phone to an employee, this otherwise usually unruffled CEO got visibly upset. His personality changed when it appeared to him that this worker was "ripping him off by doing a side job on the clock." He decided the worker was probably using paint from his company as well, and he immediately called the worker and fired him.

This worker had just received the Employee of the Month award. He was a favorite of all the managers, and he was highly trusted in his job. No matter. The CEO then called the supervisor and brought him up to date; it was now incumbent upon the supervisor to replace the guy. The supervisor strenuously objected, and the CEO threatened him with firing as well.

In the end, the whole thing proved to be a false alarm and had to be undone. The worker had actually been given the day off. The outside paint job was on his own time. Someone had pulled the alarm prematurely, and, instead of calling the supervisor, mentioned it directly to the CEO. Hard lesson learned: Your first reaction is always the worst.

Your reaction might be, "Why was this CEO even getting involved with such a minor issue? Didn't he have better things to do?" Hands-on management means something different to every CEO, but I had observed this type of irrational behavior with this person more than once. The cost to this man's company was immense as he repeatedly allowed a meme to take over and generate a panic attack. In the end, all but one of the company's key leaders, all highly trained professionals in their field, left the company over such episodes. I ended my relationship with the client as well.

What Was the Real Cost Here?

The executive experienced a chaotic episode, and that translated to a perceived loss: In his mind, he was clearly being ripped off. The worker suffered through the chaos of losing his job (albeit temporarily) and being thrown out without the respect he was due for his loyalty. The supervisor was blindsided and had to watch helplessly as one of his best workers was exposed to this CEO's irrational behavior. And as the rest of the company became aware of what had happened, the conversation that went through the organization was, "Could this happen to me one day if I'm not careful?"

So what's the cure for this reaction to chaos? It's five or ten minutes of just sitting quietly. A few minutes of reflection would have allowed him to calm down, look at the situation rationally, and make one phone call to the right person. The CEO would have uncovered the fact that this worker was on his day off. CEOs of breakthrough companies have a higher tolerance for chaos, which has a way of organizing the actions needed into a cohesive effort to stay on track.

Chaos Is the Great Transformer

Chaos has a much greater impact on complex, evolving systems, such as an organization, than it's possible to cover in this book. If you're interested in the subject, I highly recommend *Surfing the Edge of Chaos* by Richard Pascale, Mark Milleman, and Linda Gioja.[15] To give you a quick overview, here are what the authors call their four "bedrock" principles:

1. Equilibrium is a precursor to death.

2. Living things move toward the edge of chaos.

3. Components of living systems self-organize in response to turmoil.

4. Living systems cannot be directed along a linear path.

Even with these overriding principles, your organization has a complexity all its own. There is no other business like it, because it combines your thinking with that of your employees. Since there's no other you, the way you respond to events and episodes in your business cannot be duplicated.

The memes of every business are different, and the level of chaos and its impact are different in every business as well. That's one reason why you don't want to emulate or adopt another company's business model or strategy. You want your own type of chaos.

The Funnel Process

I first began thinking about chaotic discomfort when things were not going as well or as fast as I had planned. I was in the midst of innovating a new product or service, and the outcomes were harder to produce than I'd anticipated.

I would describe the struggle of that moment—the process of innovation or strategy execution—as my "funnel process." I began to notice that whenever I was on the verge of a breakthrough, I felt like I had a vise clamped onto my head, and I had a hard time sitting still. I was not allowing chaos to work.

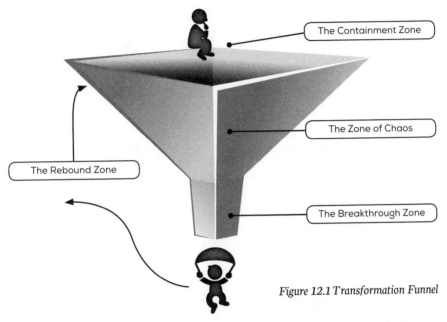

The Containment Zone

The Zone of Chaos

The Rebound Zone

The Breakthrough Zone

Figure 12.1 Transformation Funnel

Imagine a large funnel something like the one in Figure 12.1. There you are, sitting on the edge of chaos and looking into the great abyss of the inward-sloping "transformation funnel." You realize the only way to your desired breakthrough is to allow (not force) yourself to drop in and fall through.

As you move through the funnel—the process—you feel claustrophobia, as if the sides are closing in. Your natural reaction is to resist and try to get out of the situation.

What do you do? Do you then change strategies in order to feel more comfortable? Can you climb out of the funnel? Generally, you do anything you can to avoid the feeling of pressure.

I have that feeling as I write this chapter. But the difference now is that I understand the transformative value of embracing chaos. Disequilibrium is a natural feeling that comes with anything that is worth doing and doing well. So I ask myself, "Am I more committed to feeling comfortable, or am I more committed to a breakthrough?" Which is it for you? On your way through the funnel, you have a choice.

Think about a time you have been in the transformation funnel. What did it feel like? What happened?

Are you more committed to feeling comfortable, or are you more committed to having a breakthrough?

This is where the 87 percent of companies that don't execute their strategy get stuck. In the midst of the transformation funnel process, strategy gets changed or abandoned. The result is that CEOs of those companies never emerge from the funnel. They get sidetracked by the feeling of disequilibrium and begin climbing out of the funnel to start over.

The best work I have ever done—and the best work you and your organization will ever do—will occur when you literally surrender to the chaos. Allow yourself to drop through the funnel, and when you emerge at the bottom, you will be transformed into a stronger version of you. Only by moving through can you reach a place of innovation and creativity. It makes you stronger and more resilient against the sabotaging memes that infect weaker organizations.

The last thing you want to do while going through the funnel is change your strategy; that will only make getting to the end result longer. You don't have a flawed strategy. You simply need to embrace the transforming chaos.

Chaos and the Chaordic Process

Chaos has had a bad connotation for a lot of people, including me, before I understood it. When we look at the world, all we see is chaos causing trouble, as countries struggle with their political systems and Mother Nature wreaks havoc in many places on earth. When we hear the word "chaos," we quickly assume that it means some kind of painful struggle, pandemonium, bedlam, or confusion.

But chaos is a very effective tool when you want to affect the overall behavior of a complex, evolving system. Such systems are susceptible to the *butterfly effect*, which Merriam-Webster defines as

> "a property of chaotic systems... by which small changes in initial conditions can lead to large-scale and unpredictable variation in the future state of the system."

Complex systems exist in nature, in world economies, in social structures, in weather prediction, and in biological systems. Your organization is another example.

For that reason, leaders who want to build breakthrough organizations can make small changes that have huge impacts on the behavior of the business. That's the whole point of this book.

One of the ways that chaos can be transformative is through the "chaordic"[16] process. The term originated with Dee Hock, the founder and former CEO of the VISA credit card association, and it describes a blend of chaos and order that is distinguished as a harmonious coexistence demonstrating distinctions of each, with neither chaotic nor ordered behavior dominating. Chaordic principles are often used to characterize human systems like family, government, and for-profit and not-for-profit businesses.

To leverage and use chaos to transform the performance of our business—and, believe me, the outcomes can be huge—we can invent a chaordic process that takes our teams to a place of disequilibrium, which is caused by not having the end in sight.

Think about the local "haunted house" at Halloween. This popular attraction brings in mostly young people who want to experience the thrill of being terrified, even though they know that the threat is an illusion.

As you enter the house, it's usually so dark that you have trouble seeing your hand in front of your face. You bump into a few walls, and then you see a glimmer of something ahead. It's glowing, so you feel your way toward it. Suddenly a skeleton jumps out with a shriek, and strobe lights disorient you even more.

What makes the haunted house so entertaining for some is the ability to tolerate scary disequilibrium. People who don't like the haunted house experience can't stand that, especially the disturbing noises, which prevent them from being able to think through what they need to do next to progress through the terrifying maze. It's difficult to tolerate your senses being challenged in a way that throws off your ability to control circumstances. In fact, chaotic circumstances can feel physically painful, and dealing with the discomfort of disequilibrium doesn't seem like much fun either.

This explains why so many companies are managed to avoid chaos. It's like a haunted house, but it's real life, and there's no assurance that we are going to make it to the other end. What if we get lost along the way and we never see the light of day again?

How people feel about the haunted house often mirrors how they feel about life. Some people just want to get to the end; others keep coming back for more. The return visitors are the ones who are most likely to benefit from the transformative power of chaos.

Embracing Chaos Is Healthy

If you want to create an organization of innovation and creativity, you need to allow and even introduce the tension that comes with or causes chaos. Noted scientists G. Nicolis and I. Prigogine have shown that when a physical system is pushed away from equilibrium (in balance, symmetry, and stability), it survives and thrives, while if it remains at equilibrium, it dies.[17] Systems that are out of equilibrium are forced to explore their space of possibilities, and this leads to new patterns of relationships and structures. An organization that embraces chaos is healthier than one that hangs on to equilibrium, and it can achieve a new level of performance.

Years ago in my own software and telecom businesses, I needed to build an organization where creativity and innovation would move us toward technology breakthroughs. I was confident my team of talented software developers could develop the system I had come up with. I assumed I should get them to follow my thinking and produce the software that did what I was looking for. And so I held a series of meetings where I got up and told them how I wanted it done. I related my vision for an information system to alter the way people saw their organizations, and I let them know what it was going to take to get it there.

In reality, I was dealing with very talented people who could come up with innovative ways to design software that would do exactly what I wanted, but I didn't trust them to do it. My biggest fear was that if I took the time to look at any different approach to the problem, I would have to wait longer to market the software and generate revenue. I was running the business to manage my own fear of disequilibrium, thinking that if I controlled the input, I would also have control of the output. I was getting really good at avoiding the chaos that would transform the way my employees worked and give me what I was looking for. Instead, all I was creating was bad software.

There was no connection for my programmers between the issues that I was trying to solve for my customers and an actionable plan to design and build a software system that we could market to our clients that would support their growth.

I had to learn the hard way. One day one of my clients asked me to fly to Atlanta to meet with the company's management. There they told me as nicely as they could that they were losing confidence that our software would ever turn out to be what I had promised. We had sixty days to show them that the software could perform as we had promised.

Sometimes it takes an experience like this to change your perspective and open up new possibilities. I did what almost any normal business owner would do under the circumstances: *I panicked.* I flew back to Houston. I went into my office, closed the door, and I sat there in fear. Then I took a straightforward, personally confronting look at what I was doing to keep everything under control, balanced, and in equilibrium.

Just because I was the owner of the company didn't mean that I had all the good ideas. Instead of limiting the software designers, I had to let them contribute—and they did.

In the end, I surrendered to the chaos and went through the funnel— but in the process, in my fear, I had almost killed the company.

"Chaos often breeds life, when order breeds habit"

— Henry Adams

(American historian)

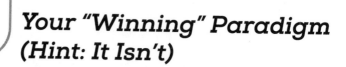

Your "Winning" Paradigm (Hint: It Isn't)

> "I count him braver who overcomes his desires than him who conquers his enemies; for the hardest victory is over self."
>
> Aristotle

> "The only true wisdom is in knowing you know nothing."
>
> Socrates

Believing Your Own Hype

Some call it ego, and some call it idiosyncrasy. It seems even the most visionary leaders at some point get mesmerized by their own success—so much so that they sometimes fall into the trap of actually believing their own shtick.

I'm continually amazed by how many great companies, led by the smartest people, plummet from their peak into the pit of paralysis. When businesses don't hold up due to conditions in the changing marketplace, most leaders realize what happened only after it's too late.

It's not that they didn't know what they're doing. Far from it: It's that they thought they had discovered their winning paradigm—the one and only model for their success—and they stuck with it for far too long. In fact, they may have been relying too much on their successes of the past to point them in the direction of a future. They acted on what they thought they "knew," believing their "success formula" to be the answer for their future as well.

Time and time again when the overly confident have to confront changes in their marketplace, many of them fail to respond appropriately—or respond at all. When they rely on the old practices of the past to respond to their competitors' new technology or strategies, their sales drop, their best employees leave, and their bottom lines shrink.

Of course, there are always a few who manage to pick themselves up, dust themselves off (and often gut their workforce), and make it back at least to some degree—though usually as a shell of their former self. But let's face it: Most do not.

Why do so many great companies fail to execute their strategies? Experience shows us the companies that fail often appear to be operating under full sail. There's lots of action, but most often it's not the right kind of action because it's what earned success in the past. Leaders think that if it worked well in the past, then it's got to work again and more of the same can only be better, and they go out of their way to convince themselves that it is working—especially when it isn't. Old-world thinking and practices aren't going to cut it in the new world of business we find ourselves in now. And you'll never become a THIRTEENER thinking this way.

Inventing a Model of Yourself for Public Consumption

We all invent a model of ourselves for public consumption. It's a formula for appearing to be winning when we fear we are not, and it's our way of maintaining some level of equilibrium in a world of chaos. But in the end, that equilibrium undermines our best intentions.

Your rigid model of yourself is a way of being that makes up for your own personal limiting perspective. It's the ideal us—what we want everyone else to see—so we display it to keep the rest of the world from finding out that most of us believe we don't know what the hell we are doing.

Whenever I've attended a networking event and asked another CEO how he or she was doing, I've almost always heard the often-rehearsed answer that things are great, or great except for some minor road bumps due to the economy. But I've never been told what's really going on in that CEO's head because appearances are so important to us. While we appear to have it all together, the conversation and self-talk going on inside us expresses doubt about who we are.

Over the past ten years, I've led workshops with everyone from CEOs of large organizations to solo-entrepreneurs, and it's the same on every level: As far as everyone else is concerned, they are doing fine. On the inside, it's another story.

To compensate for that other story, these leaders cook up the personae they want everyone else to perceive. But each such persona is the embodiment of the *pretense* of leadership (as we explored in Chapter 9), and it's what ends up running your business.

This is a problem of epidemic proportions. Your organization, regardless of its past performance, operates on a negative and limiting hidden context (a meme) that is covered up by the visible pretense of winning.

This conversation is helping to keep your company from executing its strategy, and it's holding you back from your own growth potential.

Active Inertia

I enjoy driving near my home in the Rocky Mountains of Colorado, but I have found you need to be very careful at night or you might learn the hard way about the deer, elk, and moose that cross the roads in the dark. You spot the reflection of your headlights in the animals' eyes, but they don't move, because they are literally paralyzed by the light.

I've met business leaders who remind me of deer caught in the headlights. They're suffering from a condition called "active inertia," which was revealed by Donald Sull, associate professor at London Business School, in his book *Why Good Companies Go Bad and How Great Managers Remake Them*. Active inertia, Sull says, is "management's tendency to respond to the most disruptive changes by accelerating activities that succeeded in the past."[18]

Active inertia is really a very simple concept: Entrepreneurs start companies because of a great product or service they are confident will make money. They proclaim to the market that their product or service is the "best thing since sliced bread," and the sales start rolling in. Satisfied that they now possess the formula for sustaining their competitive edge, they believe all they need to do is just keep doing what they know how to do. It's now their winning paradigm or strategy. So, that's all they do; that's active inertia in action.

When companies fall into active inertia, they get bogged down in repeating what they know and have always done. Even in the face of clear and compelling evidence that the marketplace might have already changed, they still believe and act as if they had the right answer.

Sull gives an example of this in a story about Firestone Tire Company and its reaction to Michelin Tires' new radial tire technology. Instead of recognizing the direction the market would be headed, Firestone kept its workforce focused on the old technology. As Sull says, "It just dug itself an even deeper hole."

This is a substantial problem in business. Instead of digging themselves out of the rut they're in through new practices, perspectives, and possibilities, companies end up digging themselves in deeper. To paraphrase an old saying, the smarter they are, the harder they fall. Armed with their winning strategy, companies end up victims of their own success.

When change occurs in the marketplace, these companies don't see how their thinking has undermined them until it's too late. Suddenly, they realize the competition has caught up or customers have switched to something the company wasn't even aware was needed. The company can only respond with the tried and true, thus making matters worse. The answers seem to be to do more and work harder and faster, because that's what entrepreneurs have always done.

Entrepreneurs are inventors, and inventors love what they create. They think that all they need to do is what they did to be successful in the past. And woe betide them if they were so "fortunate" as to be praised in the local press. That can make the locomotive really go off the rails.

The Telltale Characteristics of Active Inertia

Basing actions on fixed or rigid thinking from the past keeps results in the future looking like the results of the past. Haven't we all fallen into the trap of sticking with "what we know" even if it's failing to give us the result we want?

> *What has worked very well for you in the past?*
>
> *How do you foresee that a past success might turn into a future failure?*

It would be just too damn simple or ridiculous if we thought we could avoid this phenomenon altogether. It's going to happen, so the best most can hope for is to do what Joel Arthur Barker said was necessary to break out of this paradigm paralysis: "Look outside your current way of thinking and at least consider how you might be in a rut. In any authentic change effort, that's the first step."[19] When leaders begin to understand their own limiting paradigms—how what you know can prove to be the enemy—they are less likely to join the ranks of their unsuccessful comrades. Leaders should be the first to examine their own limiting perspectives.

Active inertia comes with a powerful paradox for failure. A paradox can be two conflicting ideas—for example, "I need to make a change to succeed, but I might fail." But what if failure is a good thing, and the objective is to fail so you can succeed? That's another sort of paradox. I have often reluctantly and unenthusiastically embraced new concepts in order to move forward, and the first thing that happened was that I failed. Does that mean I shouldn't try again? I have failed more times than I have succeeded, but each time I've failed, I've learned something that I needed to succeed. I needed to fail so that I could succeed.

Confronting the limiting memes in my head that produce active inertia is not always easy. If you're like me, you probably have these challenges on a weekly if not a daily basis. But taking the risk sure beats sticking with an old approach that leaves me with nothing as everyone else passes me by on their way to my future.

You need to pay particularly close attention to these telltale characteristics of active inertia.

Paradigmatic blind spots

Paradigms shape how people view the world and their business. They are the models as well as the boundaries that define our personal world. They can create a powerful context that helps leaders take their organization to the next level, but limiting and rigid paradigms can also create blind spots and restrict the ability to act on new opportunities.

Talking as a substitute for action

I point to this often in this book because leaders who "talk about it" as a substitute for action are endemic in organizations today. Too many leaders fall into the trap of allowing themselves and their employees to engage in institutionalized thinking that gives rise to faulty assumptions and unsuccessful workplace systems.

When stakeholders in the organization confuse talking about doing something with real action and nothing happens, planning and execution bog down. It's time you paid attention to this behavior. It is the chief cause of the failure to execute your strategy.

Relatedness that restricts growth

Make no mistake about it: Relatedness is the source of many of your results, and all companies should focus on it as a principle, a value, and a practice—as long as you understand how it is used in your organization. As we discussed in Chapter 10, relatedness can also evolve from a strength into an entitlement and create an excuse to justify not changing. "I want to make significant changes that would make a difference in our bottom-line results—but, I don't want to upset anyone," is a paradoxical form of entitlement-driven behavior. It generates a culture of irresponsibility in which nothing can get done because no one will take ownership.

When relatedness backfires, it's because we have treated people in a way that says they're incapable of being accountable. We treat employees like children, thinking they will love us more if we don't make it too hard on them. Give me a break! These conditions—which you are responsible for—not only restrict the organization, but they also push it into paralysis. Ultimately they result in resentment that can kill the organization.

Rules passed off as values

Dominance takes many forms. Your propensity to create rules is just a more subtle form of your own commitment to patriarchy. More often than not, the sole purpose of rules is simply to control behavior. Over time, "That's how we do it around here," creates self-defeating rules that become the focal point of the enterprise—and fodder for new memes that sabotage performance.

Rigid thinking

Rigid thinking results in false assumptions, negative assessments, and ultimately employee disengagement. Rigid thinking thwarts future intentions since it's generally tied to avoiding a repeat of a past experience. And trying to change the past results will never take you or your organization to the next level. If you want to leverage change in your favor, you need to know how the past is impacting the current thinking of everyone. It's the current thinking along with the conclusions about the past that dictate what is possible for your future.

There Are Solutions

The solutions to active inertia lie in two basic approaches:

1. **Broader participation in the process of leadership and solution design.** By creating effective teams that can create upward change, we can tap into our employees' inherent creativity, so that what we do in our workplace shows up in the marketplace with a bigger impact on the bottom line, both ours and our clients'.

Guiding a company through change of any kind can be a difficult balancing act. You have to know what critical thinking to keep and what nonsense to discard. Should you go it alone or use an outside manager who has no preconceived ideas about your enterprise? Though some argue that an outsider might be inclined to throw everything out and start over, I believe an outside perspective combined with good insider insight is what's needed. Change is best done in partnership with someone who understands how to get to the underlying conditions—the conversations—at the heart of the organization without ignoring the past and forcing the company to start from square one.

2. **Nurturing a nebulous vision of the future that has you always working to investigate possibilities on the distant horizon.** The watchword here is "distant." This should be a sort of ongoing inquiry that you verbalize but don't act on immediately.

If my client who thought he should invest $20 million into an online solution that nobody wanted had just waited a bit longer before acting, he'd be $20 million richer today. He would have discovered the solution he was actually looking for, instead of the one he built. It's important to emphasize again that context is the heart muscle of every organization. Unless you consider all the underlying assumptions and invisible premises on which your decisions and actions for the organization are based, you are S-T-U-C-K with the past.

Before you can begin to create something anew, look at the conversations in which your organization is engaged and the limiting paradigms within which people view the world and interact.

The paradigms reside in all the perspectives, thinking, and beliefs that everyone in the organization relies on and that govern the company. Remember that these are based on the experiences and feelings of the past and what those mean to people, because regardless of what management intends to communicate, everything that happens is personal to the stakeholders in the organization.

If you want to leverage change in your favor, you need to know how the past impacts the current thinking of everyone in the company. The current thinking along with the conclusions about the past dictate what is possible for your future.

To leap out of the pit of paralysis, go to work on the organization's alignment with your thinking, the quality and quantity of quality conversations, your actions, and your results. To alter the results of your organization, look at your actions. To alter your actions, look at your paradigms. At the core of it all are the conversations you are engaged in.

14

The Three-Legged Stool of Transformation: The Breakthrough Solutions Framework™ For Your Business

"Life is like an onion:
You peel it off one
layer at a time,
and sometimes
you weep."

Carl Sandburg

Defining Business Culture

Let's talk about what culture is, how it impacts performance, and especially, what theories we need to be aware of so that we can turn the lessons into practice. Principles without action are merely beliefs without application.

Often, when meeting with prospective CEO clients, I find that they are eager to tell me about their organization's culture. It's something they seem very aware of, yet when they try to describe it, they struggle. Cultures are as difficult to describe as are the characteristics of Best Place to Work companies. Most leaders and their employees just know when they're in a company that works and when they're not.

I've come to the conclusion that most leaders perceive the need for a good culture but often fail to realize that cultures, too, are functions of the conversations people engage in, in the workplace. Negative conversations (and powerful negative memes) breed negative cultures, just as positive conversations (and positive memes) result in positive ones.

Of course, a leader would want to foster a positive culture, in order to have a positive effect on executing strategy, limiting turnover, and promoting results. But how do you create a positive culture, one that gives people the empowering feeling of belonging to something meaningful?

> Let's start off by defining *culture*. Merriam-Webster's dictionary calls it: "the set of shared attitudes, values, goals, and practices that characterizes an institution or organization ... a corporate *culture* focused on the bottom line."

Since attitudes, values, goals, and practices are conversations, your organization's culture is established by the same conversations that impact the performance of your organization.

If I want people to be connected to the strategy of my organization, to each other, or to my client's needs, I need to invent the kind of conversations that will help people do that. I call these types of conversations ConnectionPoints, which I described in Section 1, and I'll discuss them more fully in Section 4. For now, the idea to keep in mind is that conversations create the culture of your business and that, therefore, you can transform your business by transforming your business's conversations. (You are already familiar with this idea from our discussions in Section 2 about replacing the negative viral memes in your company with positive ones.)

But before we can begin building a powerful workplace that reinforces our values and connectedness, we must have a foundation upon which to build. That foundation is composed of ideas that lead to lessons or skills that can be practiced, embodied, or realized. The end goal is action. And the function of foundational ideas is to take the company's vision, mission, and concepts and get them ready for action.

Three Foundational Ideas

There are three foundational ideas you urgently need in your business to transform your company into one that is not at the mercy of outside circumstances.

Transformation is *not* change. Change takes what you already have and know and makes modifications so it's the same thing, only possibly improved upon. Transformation, on the other hand, is the process by which you completely reinvent your thinking, your actions, and who you are. It's like the process of a caterpillar turning into a butterfly. A butterfly is not a better or more improved caterpillar; it's an entirely different animal that has undergone a transformation. I don't work with clients to help them be a bit better. I'm interested in looking at who they want to be (and are not yet) and then designing that.

The fastest way through the transformation process in your business is to adopt the three foundational concepts of the Breakthrough Solutions Framework (BSF) for altering the way you relate to your business future. Think of them as the legs of a stool you can calmly sit on in the middle of chaos so that you can see what you need to do to start transforming your organization.

BSF Concept #1:

Perspective Is Everything. To Transform Your Company, Transform Your Perspective of It And Your View Of Its Place In The World.

Your perspective is the view you have as you're standing in your business. To change your perspective, all you need to do is change your view by changing where you're standing—what you're standing for. If you're going to take your company to a new level of performance, it's important to first change your perspective of your business. In the rest of this book, I promise to help you do that.

I've coached many teams and individuals on this concept, but clearly I'm not a psychologist. I'm only giving you a businessman's version of how perspective works in our minds. You can interchange the words "perspective" and "view" if that helps you understand this better. How you view your employees, clients, suppliers, and competitors, is critical to performance. Even your perspective of your own role has a direct impact on you and your employees' performance.

Here's something to think about: All perspectives are made up. Your opinion and everything you think you know are made up, too. In fact, *you* made them up. Your opinion or view of everything (especially of yourself) determines how you're going to deal with it. But if your actions come from a non-reality-based perspective of the world, it stands to reason that your organization's performance might not be the best.

To change your perspective, consider how your old perspectives of your business were created: Something happened, but you didn't really see it. Your mind just matched what occurred to something that had taken place in the past. That's how you relate to it. Now you're figuratively standing in your past looking at your present. And it sets up a threat: Your past might say, "This isn't safe. Be careful; don't take any risks."

Why does it work this way? It's because your mind's chief aim is to attain safety and comfort and help you avoid experiencing anything that brought you pain and suffering in the past. This goes on all day long in business as well as in the rest of your life. This is why so many people unconsciously work to avoid failure. No one wants to go through that again, right? If you've never failed at anything, you can go ahead and disregard this. (Yes, I'm being sarcastic here.)

You're not consciously thinking about what might have happened in the past, you simply react. You may be present to the current threat, but your mind is focused on avoiding that past experience. What you think about what happened—which is different from what actually occurred—dominates your field of vision.

How does this apply to business? Accept that your current experience is filtered through your past. We can't see what's really there, we see only what's available through our limited thinking, and we end up with the limited actions available to us and, thus, the limited results.

The good news is that perspective is also easy to work with. Mindfulness plays a huge role in forming perspectives or opinions. Your principal job over the next year or so will be to become mindful of your own thinking, and when you've done that, you and your leadership team will be able to align on the perspective that best works for the future. To move your organization forward, you and your team will need to be standing together.

Enrolling them in this new way of being in business might be one of your toughest jobs. They've heard it all before. To them, this will be just the latest version of a solution. So first you have to work on yourself. **When you are successful in shifting your view of your business, new possibilities (even breakthroughs) that are impossible to see from where you're currently standing will appear as if by magic.**

BSF Concept #2:

Business is a conversation given to you by the view you have of your business, driven by your relationship to circumstances and the experience of chaos you so detest. So accept that you can't avoid the circumstances your business faces, and so instead, you need to change your relationship to them.

Business isn't at all what you might think it is. It's not a group of people getting clients to buy something and then delivering it better than anyone else. It's not better selling practices, or a better marketing plan, or a better brand. It's not just taking on a new client. Your business is made up of the conversations you engage in that dominate everything you think, everything you do, and everything (good and bad) you produce. Those conversations are at the heart of your business, yet you're not even aware of them.

Together let's uncover the conversations that are driven by the circumstances you are trying to control or change. Ask yourself *what are you committed to* that has you standing *where* you're standing in your life and in your business? Are you standing there because of what you fear might happen in your life if your business were to fail? Do you think you might lose yourself and everything you've ever worked for if you failed? Do you think that without this business, you wouldn't know who you are? Do you think your life as you know it would be over? Or maybe you believe that people wouldn't respect you or that you wouldn't respect yourself if your business were to fail? These are important questions that can lead you to understand why you won't or don't take the risk to transform something that desperately needs to be transformed.

The reason you stand where you stand—almost immobilized by fear some days—is that somewhere in the past, you saw something that terrified you, or you went through some horrible experience, or you observed someone else go through tough times, and you vowed you would do everything in your power to never experience that.

So you work every day (and most nights, I'm fairly certain) to keep the struggles of your past—the chaos—from ever recurring in your future. And you also work like hell to control the actions of the people around you so that the chaos of your past won't repeat. Actually you have fabricated the fact that the chaos threatens the achievement of your dream, but the belief has a grip on you, and it's not going to let you go.

When you wrote the email from your corner office issuing that last edict or rule, or when you sent out that biting email to your staff, you didn't do it because you thought it would help you grow or improve. You did it because you thought controlling dominating behavior would help you eliminate chaos and possible failure in the future.

So you try to control circumstances by laying down the law and by being an asshole—your employees' word, not mine. You try to control other people's behavior, and you put them through hell because you believe that will motivate them. And you feel justified. After all, you gave them a great job, and you pay them well.

However, you still haven't woken up to the fact that chaos and circumstances can't be controlled. If you learn nothing else from this book, you must come to grips with that realization. People will leave, clients will dump you, your cell phone will stop working, and the banker will not buy your "creatively innovative" loan request. But until you realize that the only thing you can do is change your relationship to the circumstances, you will be in your own living hell.

You can do a lot of things at the same time, but you can't work to avoid bad things happening to you and your business and simultaneously be working on building your organization.

You're going to have to give something up here, and you'll have to make a conscious choice: either work on keeping the past from repeating or adopt a new way of thinking and behaving.

BFS Concept #3:

All actions and results in business are determined by memes, which are specific conversations that get created internally and can either undermine and sabotage your intentions or connect your company so that it can execute your strategy.

Now we get to where the rubber really meets the road. Once you have found a new place to stand and you stop trying to mess around with circumstances and chaos, you can finally stop working hard to keep bad things from happening and making employee's lives miserable trying to control outcomes by controlling others' behavior. Once you've stopped doing those things, you can start working to transform the negative viral memes that make up the Execution Virus and Entitlement Virus in your company into positive memes that will make up the Empowerment Virus.

Negative viral memes are the products of your past experiences, and they cut off the blood supply for anything extraordinary that might be possible in your future. These limiting conversations are extraordinarily powerful, especially when you aren't aware of them and you don't know what they should sound like. Ultimately and arguably, they are the most powerful things in your life. Everything you do, everything you say in your life and in business is a function of these hidden and limiting conversations that create the context inside of which you will accomplish everything—success or failure.

Have you ever noticed how often you talk about your plans to create and accomplish something new, like a new strategy for sales? You meet with your salespeople and talk about what you're going to do differently in the future to get more business in the door. We've all had these conversations, and we've all seen these plans evaporate in the following days and weeks and never get implemented. That doesn't mean you're a loser as a leader—it means you don't understand the conversational context in which your business is operating. The plan you made was a conversation. It was a conversation about doing something differently from the way you've been doing it, and when you stood up to leave the meeting, the conversation immediately began to slowly fade away.

> **Review the three foundational ideas of the connection-driven organization. If anything seems unclear at this point, review the relevant chapters earlier in this book until all three legs of the stool are clearly in focus.**

Pay attention to this: Talking about doing anything different in the future that doesn't take into account the conversations that are already in place and running in the background means that the new conversations will always be overtaken and replaced by those older, more powerful conversations.

There's no room for your new conversation. It's like building a house on quicksand. After a while, the new conversation disappears. The old conversation simply did what quicksand does—it covers over everything.

You've got to become aware of the old, negative viral conversations that are swallowing up your efforts to change your organization's future. And then you must replace the old with new, positive viral conversations that will self-replicate and create a solid foundation upon which you can build conversations for the future.

The Blueprint for Building a THIRTEENER Company

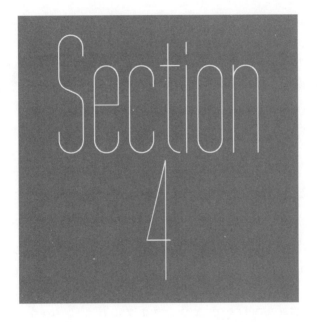

Section

4

Transforming Your Vision into Accountable Action

If our urgent undertaking is to build a business, then why wouldn't we want to build one that's considered unstoppable, one that's capable of anything we set out to accomplish? A THIRTEENER! Of course we would, but rarely is it clear what steps will actually lead to achieving that goal. If close to 90 percent of plans aren't executed, then something must be missing. What work do we need to do on the ground today to close the gap and produce the results we know in our minds are possible in the future?

This next section of the book focuses on the Breakthrough Solutions Framework™ process, the blueprint for building a THIRTEENER company. I began developing this in the mid-1990s for my own teams, and I continued to develop it after selling my two companies and beginning to advise others. I've guided hundreds of people down these steps to discover what was possible for their future. I've attempted to include all the detail you will need to understand what is required, but not so much that the process overwhelms you. There is also a "process map" for individuals and micro-preneurs, and another one for teams—all downloadable at www.ThirteenersBook.com.

Before starting the four-stage process of transforming your company with a team, I recommend you finish reading the entire book. You'll need to read the chapters on getting your employees aligned with and committed to the process, and you'll also need to learn the nonnegotiable rules of planning (Chapter 16), without which the transformation process is doomed to failure. This is designed to set you up as the leader you already are, so that you can move forward with connectedness, great vision, conscious awareness, and clear accountability.

The Objective of Section 4

In this section, I will work with you to show you how to have everything you want in your business. That is really what this book is about. Of course, there's a risk: You could try to shortcut the process and fail. I urge you to let go of all preconceived notions about planning and be open to a new paradigm in strategy execution.

The reason so many people don't achieve what they want in business is that they get in their own way. They listen largely to their ego instead of giving in to another force within themselves that has the power to give them what they want or to prevent them from reaching their goals and objectives. Think about it. The job of your ego is to get approval and admiration, get control of circumstances, get and maintain power, turn the tables, get revenge, and even the score.

Your ego is out to win. You can't do anything about that when you have no awareness of what's happening. And it's the ego's desire to win at all costs that is depriving you of a large percentage of the results you could be producing. More is possible—in your life and in your business. A great deal more. But until you are able to understand the elements that cause results in your life, you will continue to struggle.

To achieve any impossible goal, you must first surrender to the truth that you deserve to have it all. This is what is meant by "the truth shall set you free." Until you can *be* with the truth about your past, you will continue to struggle—because your primary struggle isn't with reality or circumstances. Your struggle is with your truth.

And here is the second and perhaps more important lesson: The truth requires that you become responsible for everything you have now and everything that happens to you, good or bad, regardless of what happened and when it happened. Moreover, what has happened and will happen is a result of who you are *being*, not what you're doing or have done. When you can begin to embrace this idea about your life, you will be able to find your "ultimate power," as Aristotle described it. "Ultimate power," he said, "is saying how it's going to be and then having it be that way," What we likely didn't hear him say—perhaps because we didn't want to hear it—is what probably followed: "but to have that kind of power in your life, you're going to need to be willing to take responsibility for how it is and how it isn't." In other words, you're going to need to tell the truth about your current role in how it is and how it isn't. You have 100 percent responsibility for all of it.

For most people, this is a tough concept to confront and own. Your ego would rather let you be the victim of your circumstances, focused on fighting those circumstances and thinking—falsely—you could change them if only you worked hard enough. To give up that perspective, you would need to admit you had it wrong to start with and that you're not a victim. And your ego certainly is not going to allow that. Instead, it keeps you locked into self-deprecating conversations with yourself that keep your view of yourself and your role in the world small and puny.

It doesn't matter how big your business is right now. It could just be you and you alone, or you could have a thousand employees. The primary factor that is preventing at least 87 percent of entrepreneurs, leaders, and employees from achieving their goals is their lack of awareness of the role their ego plays in undermining and sabotaging their future—your future. Your ego wants you to settle for what you have right now, to play it safe, rather than allowing you to get bigger and have something outrageous you've convinced yourself you don't deserve. Your ego has become a prison. And the key to getting you out is awareness of the truth.

In Chapters 15, 16, and 17, I will help you prepare for the transformational process. Then in Chapters 18, 19, 20, and 21, I will show you the process. (You may want to refer to the additional materials online.) And finally in Chapter 22, I discuss how you can sustain such a monumental effort with the focus on you, the leader.

15

On Your Mark: It's All in the Setup

"Trying to predict the future is like trying to drive down a country road at night with no lights while looking out the back window."

Peter Drucker

Keynote Conversations

Before you can begin to build your Breakthrough Solutions Framework™ (Vision, Awareness, Connectedness, Accountability), you will need to prepare yourself for the process. Your objective is to first enroll and then align all your employees to move together with you through the transformational process. Even before that, you need some familiarity with the kind of conversations that will make a difference in your leadership.

When it comes to executing strategy, the only thing worse than not having a business plan is having one that employees can't see themselves in, don't own, and can't execute because of the conversations that surround it and undermine it.

While crafting the right plan matters, you need to think about how to get your employees to align with you, you with them, and them with each other to be enrolled in your vision. You also need to structure the organization so that your plan can and will be executed. When the wrong people plan, the effort collapses into talking *about* the strategy, not creating a conversation *for* executing one.

I call these the Keynote conversations. They are important upfront conversations that ground you in your leadership. They are crucial to success. These Keynote conversations are part of the setup to the process. They are what I want my clients to understand, remember, and bring to the practice of strategy and execution. With them, you will create the space for success for all the members of your team—or if it's just you, with yourself.

Eight Keynote Conversations to Help Establish Connectedness in Your Strategy and Execution Process

1. **Regard the past, and then embrace the future.**
   Most of our thoughts refer to our past experiences, and strictly speaking, such thoughts usually have little or no

value in your planning process. They are often just a reaction to what has happened in the past, so that's what you end up with in your planning efforts. You get a past-based strategy that addresses your symptoms rather than the core issues that plague you. As much as possible you want to keep the past where it belongs—in the past and out of the future your plan is building.

It can be damned difficult to let go of what worked so well in the past and may feel comfortable now. And when the results seem lackluster, the first obvious solution might be to just try harder at continuing to do the things you're so good at. Resisting any kind of change is simpler—but usually less effective—than taking a hard look at what you've been doing and asking the question, "What are we missing?" What's missing creates the gap you're focused on closing in this process.

The rearview mirror offers us a clear view of the past. We can and must learn lessons from history, but as the financial industry constantly warns investors, "Past performance is no guarantee of future returns." Companies that blindly continue their strategy are likely to miss important changes within their business ecosystems as the world shifts.

Making a shift to a new, transformed way of being means letting go of what is getting in the way of growth.

Just the prospect of giving something up can be so threatening that our response is to grip what we have more tightly. Economist Joseph Schumpeter has been credited with popularizing the economic theory of creative destruction. New products and services make the old obsolete. We no longer produce typewriters, Polaroid cameras, or

Kodak film, nor do we have employee-paid employment agencies. The newspaper, publishing, travel, and music industries look nothing like they did five to ten years ago.

To transform anything, we must be open to giving something up.

Everyone knows the strategy of making money in the stock market: Buy low, sell high. However, for most of us that strategy is almost impossible to execute because our emotions get in the way. We are programmed to avoid loss. The pain we feel when our investments decline exceeds the amount of pleasure we get from their increase. We measure the loss by looking back to a time when we had more, and we measure the gain by looking back to when we had less. But we are less likely to sell our winners because we just can't bring ourselves to imagine that the future will be different. The concept is too abstract.

Your default view may be to look backward, but I will help you look to the future. Companies that fail to execute their strategies are looking the wrong way and gripping what they know too tightly, even as they plan for that so-called future.

2. **Outlaw your own opinions first, and embrace dialogue.** Remembering and spitting out facts is no substitute for thinking, and this shows up in the way we communicate. Look at the conversations going on in any meeting. They're not dialogue. They mostly consist of two things: opinions and assessments. Opinions are prepackaged ways of seeing the world, while assessments are determinations of whether an opinion fits into what the group or individuals believe to be true. This kind of communication is almost always about being right, and it guarantees you won't be the one running your company—your ego will.

However, real dialogue demonstrates the art of listening. If you're not listening, you won't be available when breakthrough ideas from your team arise. If you're not listening, you'll miss the opportunity for something great to emerge from this process. Dialogue is not just an exchange of viewpoints but a probing for clarity and an effort to align everyone by seeking and listening for opportunities to be found in alternative viewpoints. It means asking what is missing or how the situation could be made different. Real dialogue is a conversation that seeks to validate and understand more than one perspective, including those that are not yours.

In a true dialogue, all viewpoints are valid because they make sense to the people who express them. When dialogue stops, all that's available to you is a parallel monologue— people talking, very little listening going on, and no one connecting.

To create an executable strategy, you can't have people who are shut down, not listened to, and not validated for their contributions. Seeking clarification and clarity for your strategy can only occur in a safe environment, and that's not created if you're trying to win arguments or to be right. Your debate and your desire for others to accept your viewpoint simply leads to a parallel monologue that undermines and sabotages all the work you've done up to that point.

3. **Strive to think critically and imagine creatively.** For most of us, schooling just tested our mnemonic ability —how well we remembered things. Academic intelligence is too often seen as the ability to choose from a preset menu of acceptable ideas and to then respond fast. As a result, we become conditioned to want prepackaged solutions to our perceived problems. We behave as if life is a multiple-choice

test and all we have to do is find the right piece of information, slot it into place, and move on. But this is not thinking. This is the result of a past given to learning by rote.

Imaginative thinking is an experience. It requires the courage not to simply parrot back what you've read or heard somewhere else, or to rely on your past experiences, but to work with another person's ideas. That irritating self-talk that won't shut up at 3 a.m. is not thinking. Recycled thoughts can only get us so far. Ask yourself: "Who's thinking this?" and then get yourself out of the equation. Remember it's not about you.

Thinking can usefully be divided into two types: creative imagination and critical thinking. Creative imagination is open and playful and uncovers possibilities that can be put into practice and can create value, while critical thinking is alert, logical, and rigorous. Creative imagination can help us see a new way out of power struggles. Critical thinking can help us see when someone is trying to pull the wool over our eyes. It asks questions in an effort to find out whether the object of our thinking is or isn't useful.

Businesses today need to look beyond themselves and incorporate ideas from other disciplines into their planning. We need to stretch our thinking and widen our view, but we don't want to do that at the expense of self-reflection. Sure, perspective is everything, but a company infected with negative viral memes will be limited to the perspectives of only those memes. Thinking will be discouraged.

4. **Dump patriarchy.**

Patriarchy might make you think of a dour-faced man with a long white beard sitting on a mountaintop. However, it's a style of management that applies equally to men and women, and it's not pretty: There are those who rule and those who are ruled. Patriarchy creates a class divide: them and us/me.

We like to live under the delusion that class in the workplace doesn't exist, but it does. And it gets in the way of shared purpose. From the patriarchal perspective, strategic planning is status rich. That means if there are smart people who plan, there must be not-so-smart people who should just do what they are told. Yet, in a patriarchal workplace, leadership can take on cult-like status. Instead of employees wanting an environment where they can be of service and partner with others, they become obsessed with the desire for dominance. Leadership becomes the only thing to aspire to because only leaders can exercise power, discretion, and dominance over others. The patriarchal system worships the charismatic leader, whether he or she is effective or not.

The idea that each employee has something of value to contribute is missing from a patriarchal system. Employees are never allowed to be their fully human selves; instead, a leader's ego is inflated by marginalizing others. Patriarchy creates a meme-rich environment, and while there may be lip service paid to the fact that people are a company's most important asset, in a meme-infected company, talk and action rarely meet. We may hear a leader calling employees, "my people," but that implies ownership; the very language is dehumanizing. Employee potential isn't allowed or even encouraged to surface, and that's a major cause of strategy going awry.

Patriarchal leadership identifies the problem of strategy execution as either flawed strategy or flawed people; that habit of looking elsewhere for solutions removes the need for self-reflection. At the extreme end of control lies a deep-seated refusal to change.

5. **Sacred cows won't m-o-o-o-ve out of the way.**
   If the rearview-mirror approach keeps a company looking backward, sacred cows are the things that stand in the road. Everyone can see them, yet no one is going to stick a neck out to call attention to them. The sacred cow is protected. Everyone knows what's going on, but no one will say what it is out loud.

Your sacred cow may be a pet project that confers status on you the leader but has little or no business value. It could show up as favoritism and entitlement, or it could be your behavior as CEO. Take the following example. See if you can recognize this behavior anywhere in your organization, and while you're at it glance in the mirror.

We'll call the CEO Jane. She is a research scientist and medical doctor and has been to the finest universities in the United States. She comes from a prestigious family, has inexhaustible energy, and is hypercritical of anyone who does not live up to her exacting standards (which is pretty much everyone else). At meetings, she holds the floor, demonstrating her own brilliance. She never asks questions, doesn't consciously create openings for others to contribute, and never invites them to do so. Her awareness starts and stops with herself. Her leadership style demands unquestioning devotion. Those who do challenge her are humiliated, demoted, or fired. She is surrounded by yes-people.

Jane never admits to a mistake. In her mind, she is incapable of error. She takes every opportunity to assert her superiority by blaming others. In her view, everyone who works for her is incompetent. In fact, she cannot trust anyone to do his or her job. She meddles in the most mundane administrative details. Her personal assistants change frequently. Problems are met with blame and followed up with rules: "Jane's Rules," she calls them.

However, the employees do try to get work done despite Jane's meddling. They talk behind her back, and the word is that, for all her brilliance, Jane is a moron. So there are two strategies in her company that are pursued simultaneously: Do the work, and keep Jane from meddling. The rest of the staff colludes to support the dysfunctional system, but they can only do so much.

Jane is the sacred cow, with a narcissist's perspective of the future and a fear of the past. When you want others to authentically contribute, it's best to check your ego at the door.

6. **Open closed doors.**

Does your company listen to itself? How freely does information flow? Is there a secretive need-to-know policy, or is most information freely shared? Are only the values of top management considered?

People in a company infected with the negative memes of the Execution Virus are disconnected to the extent that they have no realistic perspective on the business results of their actions or inactions. In a rigid company, flexibility is seen as a weakness. Silos of knowledge never become connected to each other. Even the idea of interdependence is shunned, resulting in disconnected employees who act like cogs in a machine.

7. Accept that business is all about calculated risks— not heroism.

It is better to have enough ideas and for some of them to be wrong, than to be always right by having no ideas at all.
—Edward de Bono

Action risks failure, but one thing is certain: Without risk, there is no reward.

Entrepreneurs view risk slightly differently than most other people, and there are variations among the three main types of entrepreneurs. *Solo-preneurs* run one-person businesses, and their principal motivation for work is freedom and lifestyle; for that reason they have a tolerance for risk. *Serial entrepreneurs* are mostly interested in starting companies and selling them in the future. A main focus for this group is to attract venture capital. The venture capitalists recognize the size of the risk and knows that only one out of ten of their investments will be the big one that makes the risk worth it.

Then there are the *sustainers*, businesspeople who start a company or invest (or raise) the capital to buy a company and build it to last. They are in it for the long haul. The three types of entrepreneurs have different concerns and are motivated by different things, but they all must deal with risk.

Solo-preneurs and sustainers can easily fall prey to the meme of the heroic entrepreneur—a cultural icon that perpetuates a false, risk-loving stereotype. Yes, the entrepreneur must take risks, but these must be calculated risks. The hard work of thinking must precede action. There should be questions: Is the risk necessary or discretionary?

What are the possible rewards? What is the likely cost? What are the likely consequences? What is the cost of doing nothing?

On the other side of the coin is the company that refuses to expose itself to risk and therefore cannot take advantage of opportunities. However, always remember that there is no decision that is risk-free. Even making no decision has its risks.

8. **Reject all of the more-better-faster memes.**
   More! Better! Faster! is just another way the past would like to have a say in who you are and what you will do. It's easy to fall into more-better-faster thinking when you're looking for a way out of your current dilemma. Don't fall for these siren calls of strategy and execution. They have the potential to sink you.

"Giving back involves a certain amount of giving up"

— Colin Powell

16

Get Ready:
The Rules of Planning

"In preparing
for battle I have
always found that
plans are useless,
but planning is
indispensable."

Dwight D. Eisenhower

This chapter includes excerpts from David C. Prosser, *Peel Your Own Onion: How to Manage Your Life Like a Successful Small Business and Become Happier and More Productive.*[1]

You're set to align all your team members with your goal for transforming your company. Next you need to create the rules for the game, so that your work together leads to the execution of your strategy. I've pirated several of these rules from another guy named Prosser (aka my father, David C. Prosser) so I named them after him. Here they are:

Prosser's 11 Nonnegotiable Rules of Planning for Strategy and Execution

---

1. For planning to be relevant to your business, you must—before any work is done—uncover the hidden and limiting Execution Virus meme that is sabotaging your workplace and invent a new meme that will become the Empowerment Virus. Then you can proceed.

When I review an organization's existing strategic plan (or what the leaders might call their business plan), I often wonder what underlying conversation created this particular approach *and* what conversation might be going on to undermine it and perhaps prevent its execution. Before any meaningful planning can commence, it's critical that you take whatever time is necessary to uncover and reveal the hidden Execution Virus meme—the background conversation that will ensure your strategy is not fully executed. You must uncover and acknowledge the hidden conversation and then invent a new meme that is the Empowerment Virus. This new context will be a new place to stand, a place from which to envision the future you are about to declare.

---

1. David C. Prosser, *Peel Your Own Onion: How to Manage Your Life Like a Successful Small Business and Become Happier and More Productive* ((New York: Everest House, 1979)

This is Rule 1 because it is the most important rule and also because it is missing from almost all strategies today. Not following this rule will most likely ensure that you're among the 87 percent of companies that will fail to fully execute their strategy this year—and possibly every year.

2. You must do your own planning.

No one can do your planning for you. You can't hand it off to a team, individual, or consultant. There are corporate strategists whose job is to help leadership see what the future might be like, but they are only info-mediaries—internal information providers. Corporate planning is effective only if the corporation's top decision makers, and those who are going to be executing the resulting strategic plan, participate in generating the plan. That is because the top decision makers are the only ones who are going to have to execute it. The strategy-planning team needs to be made up of those who will promise to take action once the plan has been aligned on.

3. You must have intimate knowledge of what you're planning.

The only people who can plan for an organization are those who will have to execute the plan and who have an intimate knowledge of the organization. Yet there have been times when I've worked with an organization where a new top executive has been brought in and is at a complete loss when it comes to planning.

That person may be extremely bright, but he lacks the information to plan effectively for his new environment. Usually, an executive has to be with a company for at least a year before he or she can meaningfully contribute to the planning process. Until then, the executive can't be more than a casual observer of the nitty-gritty of the process.

An obvious example occurs in the federal government. Every two years, new congressional representatives are elected, and every four or eight years, a new president can install new cabinet department heads. These periodic changes help make government extremely inefficient. These people are simply not competent to be effective planners since they don't have an intimate knowledge of the agency they head.

Then again, there are new employees who can bring a new perspective or new paradigm to the planning process and open the eyes of the principal planners to possibilities that insiders have been unable to see. But at all times, you should include those who will be accountable for promising to act and for taking action on the strategy that you align with. If you create unreasonable expectations of employees who haven't had a hand in planning what they are expected to execute, you will be disappointed when they fail to take ownership of the outcome. Not everyone can be in on the primary planning, but part of the process is making certain that everyone is in the conversation for the possibility you have created. You do that by sharing the results of planning and by giving all employees the opportunity to *say how*, in their role, they are going to show up in the fulfillment of the outcome.

4. You must have a clear understanding of the business you're in.

The opportunity to plan for the future is also an opportunity to clarify the business you're in. For years, I saw myself in the software business. After all, what we sold our clients was software. But that's what we sold—not what they were buying from us. They were buying information that solved their companies' deep-seated issue of not having the knowledge to respond immediately to shifts in their marketplace.

Our software gathered information from disparate information sources within our clients' extended network of business outlets, and it then presented that information faster than our clients had ever seen. Before they installed our systems, they had to rely on profit-and-loss statements that became available fifteen days after the close of each month's business. By that time, they could be as much as forty-five days into a hitherto unseen problem that had started at the beginning of the month before. None of these clients cared a whit that it was our software that was doing the heavy lifting. What they wanted was to see what happened every day in their portfolio of outlets so they could respond immediately to the problems our software showed them. They were buying a daily feed of information from us.

If you're in the software business, your perspective will give you one view of the plan you need to create. However, if you're in the business of providing daily information to your clients through software, you look at your action plan much differently. Being in the software business became how we got our clients to the end result—the solution. We had to have software to deliver the information, but we didn't sell software—we sold valuable information. That was a very different business from what we had initially gone into.

Get clear about what business you say you're in. It will illuminate not only how you think of your business but also how everyone views his or her role in executing your strategy.

5. You must be committed to not bringing ready answers but instead to being willing to risk discovery and transformation.

If you think you know how your business strategy should look (even if you're the person who single-handedly started your business on your dining room table), you're also the one who will shut the planning process down so that others' perspectives will never see the light of day. And one of those viewpoints just might be the million-dollar solution you're looking for. That's a tragedy that plays out in so many businesses today. This is the reason so many non–Best Place to Work companies experience turnover of 12 percent to 25 percent and more. With every employee who feels he or she can't contribute or whose ideas are shot down, a gold mine of knowledge and experience potentially walks out the door. You can't turn planning into an adventure in exploring what's possible, if no one has a chance to make a difference or feel the pride that comes along when his or her idea is adopted. Don't be the stingy executive who won't let anyone else contribute.

6. You must be willing to experience chaos.

It's tough sometimes to just hang in there through the uncomfortable funnel process of planning. Just how do you hang in there, anyway?

First, you must be free from pressure to produce immediate results. If you're intent on not rocking the boat, or if you're not willing to have the conflicts (debate, not argument) that show up during planning, then you can expect the process to be painful at best. If you feel a need to get a plan into action, you're not going to have the time to think through what is possible in the future. Putting pressure on the process forces people to rush, and rushing brings up more about the past and less about the new future.

If you can't be in the chaos of the process, then what you will end up with is just a new version of equilibrium. And as you recall, equilibrium equals death in a complex evolving system like your business. So when the planning process gets uncomfortable, confronts you in some way, or causes you to become frustrated, step back and let people talk until you see the light again—and then proceed.

7. You must willingly be continually open to leading the inquiry of planning.

Almost every business prepares an annual budget for the coming year, and frequently, that is the sum and substance of the planning. Usually within the first quarter, the budget is shot and no longer makes any sense. The reason is that no plan in any business goes for any length of time without revisions, because new information and new knowledge are always coming in.

The information our software provided to our clients changed their plans, sometimes on a daily basis. Our clients were hotels, and what worked one week didn't necessarily apply to the next week. It was important for them to realize that constant change can be disruptive—but from a marketing perspective, when you can alter people's focus quickly, you gain competitive advantages over others in your industry.

The point is that planning never stops with the plan you align on. The Promise-Based Execution Management System process is year to year, yet each month, you will sit down and review how well you and your team are performing. Did you take the actions that each of you promised? You will measure how well you performed, and that creates important feedback and accountability. What actions do you now see that need to be taken as a result of your experiences this month that you didn't see in your first planning session? You will be planning until you drop dead—and then, when you can't plan anymore, someone else will. But it never stops. It's never, ever over.

8. You must be willing to rigorously make and keep promises.

Your execution plan will require action. This is where most plans fail. Even before you begin to plan, there must be an agreement by everyone who is intimately involved with the planning that once the plan is complete, *everyone* is committed to make promises for action and to keep those promises. This is the ongoing management of accountability that you will establish as you approach the final phase of planning. A plan without action is simply a piece of paper or a three-ring binder in a drawer or on a shelf. It's great to plan, but if you don't bring rigor to the process, your plan will be suited only for the shredder. Make certain that the people on the planning committee have a sense of urgency to see the product of their work executed. Never start planning without that first promise from your team. This is not a "let's wait and see what happens" proposition you're about to embark on.

9. Know when it's time to move on.

Getting an unstoppable plan right the first time is asking a lot. This may be the first time you've really examined who you are and what you stand for. Give yourself some space to work on issues and come back to them when there is an impasse. You can beat a dead horse, but it won't help the process. When you see that the situation has become a stalemate, move on and come back to it later. Alternatively, take it "offline" with a smaller group to resolve an issue that has the process stuck.

The way to do this is to tell the people who are stuck that you would like to set up an appointment with them to address the specifics of what can't be agreed upon in the planning session. Making an appointment may be enough to assure them that (1) you are committed to addressing the issues, and (2) the issues are important to the outcome of the process. If you take a half-day to resolve a major issue, however, your process will suffer from planning fatigue. With planning fatigue comes apathy and cynicism, which can shut down the effectiveness of the entire process.

10. You must be willing to veto anything you authentically can't support.

Along the way, there will be ideas and inspirations that come and go. If you see that something outside the realm of what you can honestly support is finding its way into your unstoppable plan for action, it's important to remain calm and ask why the thing is so important.

Allow proponents of such ideas an opportunity to defend their ideas to the entire team. The Promise-Based Execution Management System isn't intended to transform you into a doormat for anyone's ideas, so see if those ideas can stand the test of scrutiny by the entire team. Challenge the team to tell you why an idea should be in the plan for the future. If there is overwhelming support for someone's "harebrained" ideas, then perhaps you need to step aside and move on (see Rule 9). Just because there are ideas in the strategy that make you uncomfortable does not mean they should remain there. Or perhaps you do need to adjust your thinking and become more comfortable with them. Let the issue go for now. Acknowledge the person and say the idea makes sense; in other words, validate the person. The idea does make sense to the person who is proposing it, and your validation will work in your favor over the long term. If you allow your resistance to it to gush forth, you make it potentially unsafe for your employees to speak up for fear that the big bear (you) might bite them for their "stupid" ideas.

11. Make the process safe. Speak candidly and directly but never with blame. (Hint: Using the word "*you*" will put people on the defensive.)

When you're planning, there is a lot of the past to get behind you and leave there. There comes a point where you can confidently feel that the past is not going to jump out and suddenly appear to take over your strategic activities, but the threat is always there. While you are visiting the past and telling the truth about it, *never* put the responsibility on any one other person. If possible, own as *your* responsibility whatever happened on your watch. That may not be the case entirely, but what would you rather have: a planning process in which people speak up boldly to support the future of your organization or a process that is dead on arrival because people don't feel safe?

Never lay a guilt trip on employees who have agreed to participate in planning, and *never* shame them—not in public and never in private either. In any situation in which you feel there is blame for a poor choice of actions or a strategic mistake, look in the mirror to see who is the common denominator in all things that matter in your organization. If someone isn't performing, find out what the core reasons are and get off the blame game, which only addresses symptoms and not the real issues.

Remember: The real problem may be you.

"If you don't know where you are going, you'll end up someplace else."

— Yogi Berra

17

Get Set: Setting the Stage for Your Transformation

> "The roadmap for a breakthrough in business covers vast unexplored territory full of obscure obstacles and amazing possibilities, always with something new to be discovered around the next bend in the road."
>
> Daniel Prosser

Mapping the Breakthrough Solutions Framework™ for Your Company

If you look at how a house is built, there's a blueprint that provides the layout or the primary instructions for building the framework of the house. Once the framework is established, you then put on your choice of a roof, doors, windows, and walls. Then you can decorate it and move in.

The Breakthrough Solutions Framework serves essentially the same function, yet my framework gives me the flexibility to modify the final creation or outcome. It's like putting on a different roof, doors, windows, and so forth each time.

With my Breakthrough Solutions Framework I know what to expect with any client at every stage of the process. I also know that I can't build a house without a foundation. The same is true for business. I can't build a business without certain elements, like a vision.

The Breakthrough Solutions Framework was developed around five things that are missing (singly or combined) in almost every organization I have ever worked with or studied.

In Chapter 2, I introduced the concept of the "Breakthrough Solutions Framework" in a chart. In this section, I expand on the framework to provide what is missing in most organizations. This chart recaps the framework and adds new information. ➤

Recap of the Breakthrough Solutions Framework Model

BSF	**ConnectionPoints™ Promise-Based Management System** (fulfilling on what's missing in most organizations)
A New Perspective	1. An enduring **Breakthrough Vision** of the future that puts everyone on the exact same page; an invented future that empowers people, can't be forgotten, and won't disappear or go out of existence.
	2. **Revelation in Awareness** of the conversations and beliefs that undermine and sabotage Breakthrough Performance and a new Awareness of what is truly possible once the essential truth has been told.
A new Relationship to Circumstances	3. **Breakthrough Strategy** that eliminates the performance gaps and the need for survival tactics and empowers employees and other stakeholders to take responsibility for causing breakthrough results.
Conversations that Manage Connectedness and Action	4. A **Breakthrough Accountability** system that gives people back their power to produce 'real measurable results' using a new framework for boosting accountability to support what the organization is committed to.
	5. A future-based **Culture of Connectedness** that gets the constraints left by past performance out of the way of having what you say you want and create the connections people need with each other and to the activities (roles/goals/responsibilities) that are consistent with the breakthrough vision.

Steps of the ConnectionPoints™ Promise-Based Strategy and Execution Management Process

The entire ConnectionPoints PBM process can be broken into four stages in this order:

1. **Breakthrough Vision:** Declare a seemingly impossible future for you and your business to achieve.

2. **Revelation in Awareness:** Disconnect your new future from your past results and judgments.

3. **Breakthrough Strategy:** Uncover the execution gaps that need to be closed to produce results.

4. **Breakthrough Accountability:** Execute: Establish an accountability system (using the optional Accountability Scorecard™) to support you in executing your strategy and making sure all your planning doesn't disappear over time, as your old ways of thinking try to take back over.

Upon completion of the four-step process, the organization then moves into a fifth stage of building and sustaining connectedness, using the ConnectionPoints. Every organization must address each of the ten distinctions separately. This becomes an organizational dialogue that works best when everyone contributes to the process. No organization relates to these conversations alike. You may even think about using the ConnectionPoints™ conversations as your list of values.

5. **Culture of Connectedness:** Contribution, Acknowledgment, Alignment, Accountability, Communication, Relatedness, Responsibility, Integrity, Possibility, and Fun/Rewards/Gratitude.

As you move through each of the five stages, the PowerPoint questions are designed to move you closer to a final result by mapping an executable strategy that you and your team build together—or if you're a solo-preneur/micro-business owner, you can easily do this just for yourself.

Why Do I Call It Mapping?

Whenever I want to get someplace I'm unfamiliar with, I either consult Google Maps or plot my travel route on my iPhone GPS. I'm sure you do something similar. To get to where you're headed, you don't want to be running all over the place, trying to figure out the best route. No one does. So it's critical you have a map that shows you where you are, where your destination is, and the gap between here and there. That keeps you on course.

It works the same in strategy and execution. Mapping gives you the structure, and your inquiry keeps you on track for the breakthrough in the future you have declared.

The materials will you need to help you build your strategy:

1. A dry-erase board

2. Dry-erase markers in different colors

3. An easel (preferably two)

4. 3- by 5-inch sticky notes

5. Several boxes of water-based markers in different colors

6. A large format pad with tear-off sheets for each easel

7. Masking tape

8. A computer and a projector

9. The ConnectionPoints PowerPoint presentation from www.ThirteenersBook.com

At the beginning of your design day, you will distribute one sticky-note pad to each person on the planning team and put the water-based markers out. Instruct your participants, "If you are talking, you are writing." Ask them to write their answers to and comments for each PowerPoint question they're asked on a sticky note and hand it to you. Then post the notes on the board as they're handed to you, along with all the answers to each question—until people have run out of answers.

How to Set Up a Planning Session with Your Team

The first step in preparing to facilitate a critical planning session is to determine who should be involved. Smaller is better. I usually try to limit a planning session to no more than ten to fifteen people. If you need to involve more, choose the top leaders in your organization and plan to involve the remaining people once the top level of leadership has done the first round of planning. Other alternatives in a larger company are to take your division or department heads through the first round and train them to conduct the next round with their own direct reports. I've written a process map for this purpose. You will find it at www. ThirteenersBook.com.

Next, find a great place to conduct your planning session. Somewhere off site is always great but not necessary.

Third, set a date approximately two to three weeks to a month ahead to allow people to clear their schedules and to give you time to survey them. You can write a short invitation (not a demand or an order) asking them to join you in your planning session. You can download a sample invitation for free at www.ThirteenersBook.com.

Fourth, conduct a ConnectionPoints™ Employee Survey to better understand your organization's current thinking. This survey is based on ten two-part questions that help to uncover the issues and concerns of employees. It's a confidential survey that lets people feel safe as they tell you what's really happening in your workplace. It will indicate where the weak areas are in your employees' perspectives of your organization, and it can help you begin to uncover the viral meme that has infected your organization.

You can access the ConnectionPoints Employee Survey at www. ThirteenersBook.com. Download the questions and use Survey Monkey (www.surveymonkey.com) or another online survey tool to set up and distribute the survey anonymously to your entire organization. To get a better understanding of who thinks what, launch two surveys: one for your executives and one for all other employees.

Alternatively, if you prefer to have your survey administered by an independent party, you can purchase this survey from www.ThirteenersBook.com and have it independently launched and an analysis prepared for you before your planning session. Plan on a ten- to fifteen-day turnaround.

The ConnectionPoints Employee Survey asks a two-part question that covers both sides of the same issue, and it asks the respondent to answer using a seven-point Likert-scale questionnaire. For example, the first part of each two-part question asks how well you as an organization manage a particular conversation within the workplace. The second part asks the employee to rate how important he or she believes that conversation is to the organization's future. The result is two numbers, and the difference between the two will identify for you the gap in that particular conversation. Thus it will show your weaknesses and strengths in these important areas that contribute to performance.

Additional Preparatory Materials

Before beginning an important session with a client's team, I like to find a way to ground the team in a new way to approach their work together. For that, I use a DVD to start my team sessions titled *Celebrate What's Right with the World* hosted by Dewitt Jones. Another DVD that has been extremely helpful in communicating the important distinction of paradigm shifts is *The New Business of Paradigms, Second Edition,* hosted by futurist Joel Arthur Barker. I first saw the original version of Barker's DVD in about 1976. Its message has stuck with me for decades.

You can buy or rent a copy of either or both of these powerful DVDs from www.starthrower.com. (Tell them I sent you, and they may be able to provide you with a consultant's discount.)

If you download the ConnectionPoints PowerPoint (see the last item on the materials list), you can simply follow the PowerPoint through the process. However, I recommend you familiarize yourself with the process, the questions, and the PowerPoint before you start.

For a formalized workbook for each member of your team, you can order team member workbooks at www.ThirteenersBook.com. You can also order workbooks that are personalized with your organization's logo, along with a personal letter from you inside the cover, all for a small additional charge. Be sure to allow a few extra days for customization.

To Create a New Future for Your Business, Ask Questions, Then Listen

The ConnectionPoints process uses the Socratic method of inquiry and dialogue, combined with Appreciative Inquiry. Both of these rely on investigation as a tool guided by questions. The process is designed as a series of requests for the sharing of information and dialogue. Here's what I'm talking about:

- The **Socratic method** is based on asking and answering questions to stimulate critical thinking between individuals with contrasting and sometimes divergent viewpoints and to illuminate ideas. It is a process of searching for general, commonly held truths that shape perspective, and it allows participants to scrutinize these truths to determine their consistency with other perspectives.

- **Appreciative Inquiry (AI)** is the cooperative search for the best in people, their organizations, and the world around them. It involves methodical discovery of what gives a system "life" and when that system is most effective and capable in economic, ecological, and human terms. AI involves asking questions that strengthen the capacity to heighten positive potential. It mobilizes inquiry through crafting an "unconditional positive question," often involving hundreds or sometimes thousands of people.[19]

Socrates claimed to know nothing. Instead he asked questions and used dialogue to create and share knowledge. He sought to discover and teach universal truths, and he insisted that all people had knowledge within them.

How often have you taken that approach with your team? Have you ever been willing to put your opinions and assessments aside and defer to the thoughts, reasoning, and knowledge of your subordinates? It's difficult. If you've been in business any length of time, you might have learned to trust yourself, and you might often doubt the wisdom of others, especially if they don't have your experience. Perhaps you've had to cajole them into taking action.

You probably have great employees who work their tails off, but how often have you turned the thinking over to them and listened? Now's your chance! This process works when you honor and respect the contributions of others.

At the same time, when was the last time you asked questions that drew out the best in people, rather than trying to pin a problem on someone on your team? Too often your frustrations with outcomes get the best of you, and you can't help but ask questions that point up an individual's weaknesses instead of the strengths on which you could build a better company. Trust me, I've been there, too.

Remember when I said, earlier in the book, "Perspective is everything"? The view you now want to create with your team is one that emboldens people, lifts them up, makes them feel like heroes, and elevates their hard work. In the ConnectionPoints process you are asked to identify experiences of the past that have resulted in outcomes that worked. This is the AI approach to strategy creation. You find the good and the great to build on, and then you debate the nuances until you've finally crafted a powerful place to come from—*to come from*—not a place you have to work like hell to get to by tearing down everything that didn't work. A powerful stand will keep your future front and center.

LET'S GET STARTED!

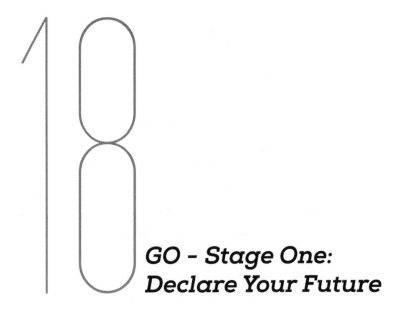

GO - Stage One:
Declare Your Future

"There's no present.
To have more than
you've got, become
more than you are."

Jim Rohn
(entrepreneur and
motivational speaker)

Transformation Begins Here

Stage One is the beginning of the end of equilibrium and balance. In this stage, you do the following:

- Break your ties to your thinking that recreates your past or some semblance of it. You are closing off the past as your source of understanding.

- Declare and map the future you are committed to bring into existence. You get to *say how* here.

- Declare what is ultimately possible in that future, even if you're not sure.

- Identify what overall outcomes you will commit to— bold outcomes only.

Stage One Is the Genesis of a New Future for Your Organization.

Leading Stage One

In Stage One, you allow your team to say whatever is necessary to "be complete with" the past, to invent, as a cohesive team, a future not constricted, hampered, or informed by that past. To be complete with the past means that nothing from the past is negatively informing any possible future. To get there, you inquire into the current "truths" that people have made up, spread around, believed in, and even gossiped about. In other words, Stage One is where you start uncovering the source of the viral memes that make up the Execution Virus in your company.

It's crucial for you to keep in mind that the truth for you may not be the truth for others. You need to be prepared and willing to hear any perspective they have about the past, and you must tell them you are willing to hear it all. When I say, "perspective is everything," in this case, I'm pointing to each person's perspective that impacts the conversations (and outcomes) they have about what doesn't work about you (especially you) and your company. Any possibilities for those conversations changing are dependent on your being willing to listen and remaining unattached to what people believe, feel, or judge.

When I have taken my own teams through this process, I have had to emotionally (not physically) leave the room. Of course, I'm not walking out, but it's critical in this stage for you not to get defensive. Don't get attached to your own perspective. Hold your tongue and remember this: Just because someone has an opinion or a made-up assessment of how things don't work in your company, that isn't the *final* assessment of your company. Your job is to listen and not respond and get the negativities spoken and complete. If you fight against what anyone says, you literally cement it in the space you're trying to clear out.

Do not respond to employees' perspectives or perceptions of "how it is" for them. Just because they see it that way doesn't mean it's the truth. It can be their truth without your having to correct it. The real truth will come later, as you will see. Trust me here.

In the first stage of this process, you will be confronted, I promise you. I beg of you not to respond from your old way of being the boss. It won't be helpful to what you want out of this work. Your first defensive outburst objecting to someone's perspective will make the rest of the process much more difficult than it needs to be. Just relax and hear what they have to say. Make it safe for them to get it all out.

As I've said, this is your chance to create the safety that your employees need to have in order to be able to authentically and fully contribute to amazing outcomes in the future you're about to invent.

When you take the time to get everything uncovered about the past—both good and bad—and when you validate that information regardless of your own opinion of the truths of other people, you create a safe place to say anything.

I once employed a controller who, I discovered, didn't want to give me any bad news. I told him that he needed to tell me what was happening in the company financially if I wasn't aware of it. Apparently he didn't want to disappoint me or get me upset. He was really a nice guy, but I had to fire him because he was essentially giving me no information—and no information is bad information.

I want to be clear with you that I know now that this was *my problem*, not his problem. I didn't make it safe for him to tell me bad news, and I apparently wasn't willing to hear it, or he wouldn't have withheld it. Don't make my mistake. I lost a good controller. Look at the people on your team and tell them that you want to hear all their perspectives—every bit. You don't want them to hold anything back. Tell them that you won't penalize them for their viewpoint. Then dig in for the ride. You will uncover the source of all your current results when you're willing to hear what doesn't work, especially when what doesn't work is about you.

Again, as I've said, the key will be how you behave when you hear what others have to say. It may be the truth or not. That doesn't matter. From their perspective, it's their reality. Here's another technique to consider if you want an even more powerful outcome for the day—mirror and validate. Once you hear what people on your team have to say—even if you can't make total sense of it, remember it makes sense to them, and you want to validate *that*—listen carefully and mirror back exactly what you heard them say. That's the mirroring part. Then tell them, "That makes sense." That's the validation part. You can acknowledge that it might have been hard to share that particular information. They might fall out of their chairs when they hear that.

What you're essentially communicating to them is (don't say this part out loud), "What you personally have to share is appreciated, and your perspective is acknowledged and valid. It's your perspective, and for that reason, you are essential and valuable to this process." If you respond that way, by the time you have validated each of the first positive and negative responses to your question, you will have begun shifting the context of your relationship with your employees.

This is the first critical step in the real transformation of your organization into an unstoppable company. I learned this technique of mirroring and validation from Dr. Harville Hendrix. His process of dialogue has made a huge difference in my own and my clients' effectiveness.

Transformation, Not Change

This is a process designed to activate transformation, so before starting, let's once again be clear about the difference between *transformation* and *change*. Change is just the alteration of something you already have. You take something in existence and create a new version of it, but it's still the same old thing. For instance, if you are struggling with sales, you might look at your sales plan and change the kind of clients you call on or hire new salespeople with different skills. But you're still using the same thinking that went into the original plan, the same way of being in business, now altered slightly with the hope of a different outcome. That's change.

In business, the outcome of change is simply a more, better, faster approach to what you already have. What you want is something completely different.

Transformation is not change. It's the creation of something from nothing. It's causing into existence that which did not exist before. Transformation is borne of the creation of a possibility—a declared outcome with no evidence that it is even possible—a desire for, and a commitment to, something that is not already.

The First Four Steps Toward Transformation

It is said that a journey of a thousand miles begins with one step, but I'm going to go above and beyond here and give you the first four steps.

Step 1: Break with the past

The first step in the ConnectionPoints process is to make a complete break with the past, and the only way I have ever found to do that effectively is to acknowledge what happened in the past and tell the truth about it—the good, the bad, and the ugly. When you ask your team members to describe five or six events from the past year that boosted their spirits or that they are proud of, they are immediately disarmed. They expected you to start your planning by launching into what's wrong with performance and, by association, what's wrong with them. Do the opposite by leading off with the good, and that will set the tone as you work together on aligning on your new future. It will help you deal with the bad and the ugly in due course.

There will always be some good in your past that works for you and that you keep. But past-based thinking is limiting and simply reestablishes the past's power over you. You want to break ties with that past so you can invent something new.

The biggest perpetrator of nonperformance is the way you as a leader treat those who are subordinate to you. This is your golden opportunity to change the way you behave—by visiting all the past things that you can celebrate with your team and all the things that help you see what's not working for you to work on later.

Step 2: Declare and map your future

Declaring and mapping your future is the first step in shaping what is not already (nothingness) into what is desired (somethingness). Changing your strategy (what you have) will not create the future you want.

Now is the time to start digging into the notion of who you *are* for the world.

Mapping the future is about the design of ideals, principles, and values. It's these factors that determine how people will view you in the future—and how you will view yourself. By itself, a map of the future is just words. But when you take those words and create your impossible vision for the future, you will have a powerful platform to launch any project and produce any outcome you desire.

Your declaration of the future is called a vision, not a "for certain." It's a vision of a possibility, and that possibility opens up opportunities. Mapping the future is the tool for shaping what is not yet created and may not seem possible from your current perspective. You are shaping it into a brand-new way of looking at the world—your new perspective. With your vision, you're beginning your journey through the funnel, through chaos, and through disequilibrium. It's got to be big and bold enough that it will cause you to actually struggle with it as a possibility.

What is the declaration of the future that you are committed to and that represents who you see yourself being as your future unfolds? Can you put it into a few words? My own vision for the future will never be attained.

> *I'm committed to the possibility of a world where people love what they do and have what they want in every dimension of their lives.*

Will the world ever see that? Probably not in my lifetime and probably never, but it's *my* vision, my stand for what's possible, from my perspective. It expresses a possible future I'm committed to. It's what drives this book, all the work I do with clients, my courses, and my software.

The impossibility of it makes it big enough—bigger than me for sure—to be worthy of my efforts. It calls me to *be*; everything I am focused on is in service to that vision of the future.

Steps 3 and 4: Declare what is ultimately possible in that future, and identify the overall outcomes you are committed to

So, what future would you be willing to have? I mean really willing. Even if you can't actually see yourself there, where would "there" be? Swing out and think big. Thinking is free. Can you imagine something that your mind actively resists envisioning? Listen to yourself, because that is the future you want to create.

When you say to yourself, "Oh, I can't do something like that," then you know you're on the right track! Perhaps you're being held back by a concern for what others would think of you for envisioning this future. How many people do you think told Steve Jobs he was crazy to think he could build [insert any Apple product here] or told Howard Shultz he was crazy to think he could sell coffee for several dollars a cup, change the way people build community, and change the way farmers sell commodities? These two guys changed the world for all of us with crazed notions of what was possible. Believe me, if they were able to do it with their crazy ideas, you can, too. There is nothing they can do that you can't. "Can't" is not a word for this work.

When to Move On to Stage Two

In Stage One of the ConnectionPoints™ Promise-Based Execution Management process, you break ties with the past because that past can't comprehend something called a future. Let go of your fears and limitations, and invent a new possible future for yourself and your company, one that will likely scare you. Stop listening to your past.

You can look at Stage One on your downloaded Process Map.

You're ready to move from Stage One to Stage Two when you have identified a vision for your future that is not possible to imagine in your current world.

19

GO - Stage Two: Disconnect from Your Past

> "For the past 33 years, I have looked in the mirror every morning and asked myself: 'If today were the last day of my life, would I want to do what I am about to do today?' And whenever the answer has been 'No' for too many days in a row, I know I need to change something.'"
>
> Steve Jobs

The Discovery Stage

In Stage Two, you begin to venture into your past so you can tell the truth about it and—most important—release your attachment to it. For now, your future looks exactly like your past, but that is going to change.

Here's what you will do in Stage Two:

- Reveal the conditions underlying all effort and results.

- Take the curse off the future, putting everything on the table for questioning, challenging, and revealing.

- Discover current results.

- Discover current thinking, beliefs, and perceptions behind current outcomes.

- Discover the negative viral meme that's undermining and sabotaging employee performance (your Execution Virus).

We are all challenged by this nebulous thing called the future. The *future* is the indeterminate period of time that follows the present. Its beginning is predictable, owing to the reality of time and physics. We don't question it, yet it confounds us, and when we don't arrive at the future we anticipated, we often feel thwarted. It becomes an unfulfilled expectation or an anticipation that was not delivered on.

Consider this short passage from the poem "To a Mouse, on Turning Her Up in Her Nest, with the Plow" by Robert Burns:

> The best laid schemes of mice and men
> Go often askew,
> And leaves us nothing but grief and pain,
> For promised joy!
> Still you are blest, compared with me!
> The present only touches you:

But oh! I backward cast my eye,
On prospects dreary!
And forward, though I cannot see,
I guess and fear!

Burns expresses a farmer's regret and apologies to a lowly mouse for plowing his field and cutting through its nest in the cold days of December. He feels he failed the mouse, but he recognizes that perhaps the mouse probably doesn't view it the way he does. The mouse does not condemn the farmer for what was an unintended mistake—something totally outside the control of the mouse that disrupted its future.

Your future is not predictable, yet while preparing for your future, you may forget to enjoy your experience of the present moment, something that Burns believes the mouse is fully capable of and that he, Burns, is not. I doubt the fear of the future impacts the lives of any other creature on earth besides us humans. It literally dominates us. Oh, to be a mouse!

The farmer reminisces on "prospects dreary," or bad events that have happened in the past, which he opines prevent him from making progress because he is fearful of repeating mistakes. When you are concerned about the past repeating itself, you hold yourself back not only from entering your future but also from experiencing your present.

As I've said, it's difficult to not be focused on the past. It's more comfortable that way because it's all you know. It's all your employees know. By hanging on to the past a bit longer, you think you can avoid the discomfort of risking the present/past for the possibility of a much bigger future that you fear you may not be able to pull off anyway.

It's easier to just settle for what you have and never venture out of the safe place that allows you to hang on to your false sense of security. All for what? So that you don't have to face the fact that you are vulnerable to failure if you take risks? But your ability to produce breakthroughs in your business requires that you experience failure. You need to understand that on the other side of every failure, a breakthrough is waiting. If you accept that, you'll eagerly await more failures so that you can experience more breakthroughs. To get there, however, you have to be willing to risk your past for a more powerful future.

Are you willing to do that? Right now, maybe not so much. But you'll get there in Stage Two.

Mapping Your Present/Past

The fear of repeating the past runs the lives of almost all business leaders, and it explains why you don't have the results you want. If you're unwilling to let go of your past, then that's what you're going to have to settle for. But creating a future is a lot simpler than your past would mislead you to believe. The negative viral memes that make up the Execution Virus in your workplace are a reflection of your past. If only you were saying those memes out loud rather than being unconscious of them, they would have no control over you and the execution of your strategy.

The good news is that when it comes to getting your negative viral memes under control, the old adage "Sunlight is the best disinfectant" applies 100 percent! Exposure of your memes is the most essential part of the process of disconnecting from your past so it won't dominate your future.

Right now, you might want to make this your mantra: **"There is no past. There are only the conversations I have about the past that dominate my actions and thwart the future I say I want."**

Up until now, the past and the memes it has produced in your workplace have had all the power to determine your outcomes.

You can look at Stage Two on your downloaded Process Map.

Once you've completed Stage Two, you will have your power back.

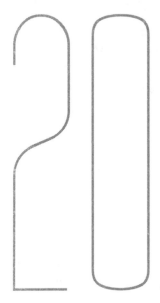

GO - Stage Three:
Mind Your Gap

"Look for what's
missing. Many
advisors can tell
a President how
to improve what's
proposed or what's
gone amiss.
Few are able to
see what isn't
there."

Donald Rumsfeld

Preparing to Lead Stage Three

Here's what you will do in Stage Three:

- Uncover what is missing that, if it were present today, would cause your invented future to be fulfilled.

- Determine the missing strategies and processes that you must implement to close the gap.

- Determine the human assets that are missing in your organizational structure.

- Determine where trust and safety are missing.

Some of these steps involve being able to identify a reverse salient. *Reverse salient* is a military term. It refers to a backward bulge in the advancing line of a military front. Imagine an army advancing on its enemy in a bowed-forward formation. At any point in that formation, if the enemy establishes a stronghold and is able to push part of that advancing front backward into itself, it creates a reverse salient. A reverse salient causes the forward progress of the military front to slow or stop; it can even put the whole army at risk of collapsing. When this happens, the generals usually pull together resources to address this weakness and bring the reverse salient back in line with the rest of the front. Reverse salients have a way of getting the attention of leaders.

Now let's apply this concept to your business. Reverse salients are the weaknesses in the systems we operate within, and more important, they are where opportunities are located. Without identifying the reverse salients, many innovators in business would not have been able to see where to focus their efforts to create the amazing world we live in. Identify these weaknesses in your business, and you have the foundation for making progress within your organization and for focusing on the innovations that will give you the greatest opportunity for success.

Thomas Edison was perhaps one of the most prolific observers of reverse salients. We often think of him as the inventor of the light-bulb, but in fact, at least a dozen other inventors did that before him. What Edison recognized was the opportunity to improve upon the incandescent lightbulbs that had already been invented, and he did it in response to a reverse salient: the problems of filament burnout, short life, expensive production, and the impracticality of the invention's large-scale commercial use. In 1879 Edison solved the reverse salient that made it possible to use an incandescent bulb to light the world.

To bring the reverse salient concept into the present day, a new future for any organization is not possible without identifying a gap, a breach, or an opening that a new future will emerge from. Without this gap, which only you can generate, only the past is possible because nothing is needed or wanted; there are no reverse salients. If it's not possible to perceive a gap, then there is nothing for you to cause into existence. Transformation begins and ends in the gap you create and stand inside of.

Mapping the gap is one of the most important elements for executing a future-based strategy. Now that you've identified the future you are committed to (Stage One) and you've cleared the past out of the equation by telling the brutal truth about it (Stage Two), you can begin to explore your gap. You want to lower yourself into the abyss—go through the funnel, step into the gap, and find out what's missing that you couldn't see while negative viral memes were running the show.

You can look at Stage Three on your downloaded Process Map.

*"I have not failed.
I've just found 10,000 ways that won't work."*

— Thomas A. Edison

21

GO–Stage Four: Establish Real Authentic Accountability

"Accountability means walking the walk once you have talked the talk."

"Accountability is integrity."

"Accountability is the ability to follow through with your commitments."

Yale students, 2007

"Sweating the Assets"

In Stage Four, you will analyze, understand, and negotiate new processes. To accomplish that, you will do these things:

- Establish and reinforce ConnectionPoints™ values, processes, and practices—which place service over self-interest.

- Determine the priorities for staying on track.

- Determine the promises for action.

- Determine the criteria for satisfaction and who will manage satisfaction and hold people accountable.

- Establish the ongoing use of the Accountability Scorecard (available online at www.ThirteenersBook.com).

The outcome of business operations is the harvesting of value from assets owned by a business. Assets can be either physical or intangible. An example of value derived from a physical asset, like a building, is rent. An example of value derived from an intangible asset, like an idea, is a royalty. The effort involved in "harvesting" this value is what constitutes business operations cycles.

Typical business operations encompass three fundamental management imperatives that collectively aim to maximize value harvested from business assets:

1. Generate recurring income.

2. Increase the value of the business assets.

3. Secure the income and value of the business.

This has often been referred to as "sweating the assets."

One of the greatest unrecognized assets of your business is an act of speech called "A Promise to Take Action." Have you ever considered a promise to take some kind of action as an asset, let alone valued it as such? Probably not.

Yet people in your company are making promises all day long. There are overt promises that people agree to make, and then there are the actions they take to fulfill their promises. Promises are intangible assets. How effective are you at wringing the value out of them?

The Accountability Struggle

Wherever there's a struggle with the practices and principles of "accountability," I've noticed the culture of the company becoming drained of its energy. A lack of mastery in accountability means everything is up for grabs. When accountability is weak, so is your ability to compete effectively.

When no one can tell the truth about what is and isn't happening, when no one can hold others to their word, when people can't be counted on, and when accountability isn't implemented, then integrity is lost, and you can end up creating a negative viral meme that undermines performance.

Results of Poor Accountability Practices

Organizations with poor accountability practices have the highest failure rates in business, and they have the greatest difficulty achieving the results they want and need—let alone the ones they've created a strategic plan to achieve.

It's not that people don't want accountability; it's just that it's probably the most misunderstood practice in business. That explains why good accountability practices are missing to one extent or another in just about every single organization. And it's why at least 87 percent of companies are not executing their strategy. If you want your company to become a THIRTEENER, you must master accountability.

What Is Accountability?

What does it mean to be accountable? Put differently, what does it mean to be count-on-able? Few people really know; and implementing accountability is a struggle when we don't even know what it is.

It starts with leadership. How can any organization hope to accomplish its mission when the leader struggles to get people to commit to take action and then fails to hold them accountable when they don't? What do you imagine that does to the future of your company?

Ninety-five percent of CEOs have some plan for achieving growth and profit this year. Every business leader has a vision for what's possible in his or her business—or at least you do now. Otherwise, you may be wasting your time in business. Perhaps you're struggling with how to achieve your vision—or with getting your employees to contribute to achieving it. If you're ever going to achieve your vision and accomplish your mission, you're going to have to rely on other people who commit to helping you get there. If people don't keep their promises to do their work and there is no accountability for nonperformance, then low expectations, mediocrity, and failed goals take over.

It's Time to Rock the Boat

CEOs and entrepreneurs like you are often the most creative breed of business leaders. You think differently than everyone else. Most of you are people oriented; you love the people who work with you. Some of your employees are your best friends; you may have even hired them because they are. You certainly don't want to upset the most important people in your life. You want to get along with everyone. And you want them to like you.

Perhaps those relationships helped you establish your company, and some of your current employees sacrificed to help you achieve what you have. Unfortunately, all of this can lead to problems in establishing accountability.

What I often hear is, "How can I now ask them to stand up and make promises and then get on their case when they don't do what they said they would? I know it's a bad precedent to set, but I don't want to lose my best and most loyal employees. If I ask them to be accountable when they don't perform, they'll leave. Then what will I do?"

How can you produce the kind of results you need when you don't know whether you can count on people and you're worrying about offending them when they let you down? How can you plan for the future if you don't think your teams will be able to get you there? What kind of plans will you come up with for a team that may or may not take action? What happens to your integrity as a leader when you don't handle the critical issue of accountability?

When you structure your relationships in business around individuals rather than around accountability, performance suffers. Your relationships not only end up costing you financially when the job doesn't get done, but also those same relationships will suffer if you settle for mediocre performance. When promises to perform are excused, you become "reasonable." Resentments build, and unresolved problems have the potential to make things much worse.

How can you turn this around and make accountability work for you and your employees—*especially for you?*

Sweating the Assets

"Sweating the assets"—which I defined earlier in this chapter—is not a new term. It seems to be a lost concept from long ago.

If you have developed a new way to solve an old problem, the model for that solution is recognized as intellectual property (IP). IP is inherent in the form of information used to transfer value to the user or client. You have likely invested extraordinary amounts of money—and emotional currency—in the development of your IP, and if someone were to copy it, you would do everything in your power to protect it, even if that meant taking the matter to court.

Therefore, an asset doesn't necessarily need to be represented by a number on the balance sheet. For example, it's hard to value your employees or your distribution channels or your IP on a balance sheet. In the same way, you can't assign a monetary value to what people say they are going to do. Yet, in a real sense, a statement, such as a promise to do something, is one of those high-value assets that often is overlooked. If it is written in a contract, you have the solid evidence of a promise being fulfilled as a future asset. But contracts only rarely appear on the balance sheet as an asset—the outcome does, but not the promise itself. It probably has not been your practice to focus on "harvesting" a promise's value because we tend to overlook that. As a result, we rarely manage that asset very well. But, as with any asset, a promise will either increase or decline in value depending on how well it is managed.

"Sweating the assets" means we take existing assets (and that includes promises) and find ways to add value to them so that they grow and produce a new return.

A good example of sweating tangible assets comes from Canadian Pacific Railway. Several years ago, this company was looking for ways to expand into a commodity transportation business because the paradigm had shifted to airline travel. It discovered it had a moth-balled fleet of vintage rail cars. So it fixed up those cars to re-create the era of 1920s luxury and began offering coast-to-coast high-end rail travel. The company took an asset with little apparent value, added value to it, and produced a greater return on that asset. It sweated its assets.

Southwest Airlines did the same when it found itself losing revenue. Instead of buying better airplanes or new equipment, it looked for assets—some of which were intangible—to help them produce better value for their customers. What was born was a new process for moving bags using existing equipment, which led to the ten-minute turnaround. By sweating its assets, Southwest discovered unrealized value inside the organization.

Inventing Accountability

Accountability is a function of alignment; they go hand in hand. If you find there's no alignment, there will likely be no accountability. If there's no accountability, there's a pretty good chance there will be no alignment.

Accountability most likely has *not* been missing from your organization in the past, even though you may believe it has. Here's why: Something can't be missing if you haven't perceived it in the first place. But going forward, there's a new slate for accountability.

To create accountability, you need to get comfortable with the idea that there's nothing wrong; there's nothing to fix.

If you don't understand accountability, it's not missing. Accountability is invented at the point that people declare their alignment to a mission and assert their commitment to the result that's desired.

Getting Clear on the Mission

Accountability is a function of what people say is important to the outcomes for the organization. This requires both employees and leaders to be clear about the company's mission, and in many cases, that's highly unlikely. In a study of employees and managers I read several years ago, it was reported that only 5 percent of all employees—managers included—knew the mission of the organization they worked for. A lack of accountability naturally followed. After all, it would be difficult to hold someone accountable for contributing to your mission if he or she weren't clear about the mission in the first place.

Three Distinctions: Accountability, Being Accountable, and Holding People Accountable

Company breakthroughs are only possible when you know the principles and practices of accountability. You need to be aware of several distinctions, beginning with **accountability** itself. This might be characterized as the actions that people are assigned that would be consistent with the mission of the organization. For example, if it is the mission of the organization to provide services, then it is someone's accountability to make sure team development, marketing, sales, service, and so forth, are in place.

Accountability Reports to Accountability

Accountability breaks down when we stop relating to others according to their accountability, the role they play in the workplace. This is where things go off track and actions come to a halt. If you relate to another person as your work buddy or a friend, rather than honoring that person's established or declared accountability, then it is very difficult to hold that person accountable. There is always a reluctance to step on that person's toes.

Accountability should create a gap (read: reverse salient) that causes people to expand into it. If I'm the team leader, and I create accountability, that requires me to grow and, in turn, that should cause everyone who reports to my accountability to have to expand and grow as well.

Being Accountable Means Being Count-on-able

This is where measurement comes in. Being accountable is not *doing*. In fact, accountability per se is really not something you do. You can *do* something all day long and not be accountable for the results.

Being accountable requires that people **be count-on-able**. This means making promises and keeping promises. People who are count-on-able are good for their word. They do what they say they will do.

Holding People Accountable Means Holding Each Other Accountable

Holding people accountable requires that we hold each other accountable for promises made, not just that a boss holds his or her employees accountable. In a connected organization, everyone holds each other accountable for fulfilling promises. It takes rigor and a willingness to look like the "bad guy" to keep integrity in the organization: If a person promises to produce a particular result, someone (or a team) holds that person accountable for fulfilling that promise. It requires saying, first, "You said this, but you didn't do this"; then, declaring what's missing; and, finally, requesting a promise to clean up the situation (or renegotiating the original promise). No shaming involved.

These aspects of accountability are missing in just about every organization I've known. It takes some effort to achieve a high level of accountability, and you have to be careful not to establish accountability in a way that sets people up for failure. It's best to determine the most important areas where you need to distinguish accountability and then to slowly and deliberately grow it in those areas. Wholesale, radical change of the way you deal with accountability will not work even for the most transformed organization.

Here's what I want you to leave this chapter with:

- A new method to distinguish accountability for yourself so you will know what you're working toward

- The capacity to ask your team members to be accountable, so that they willingly step up to the plate to sign up for accountability in your organization

- The knowledge of how to get on the right track in your relationships at work so you become responsible for results

- The understanding that accountable leaders are good stewards

- The five elements of accountability, which I call the Five Steps to Effective Promise Management

Closing Your Accountability Gap: Effective Promise-Based Management

Organizations with clear intentions of high performance—of reaching or even exceeding the goals and objectives they set for themselves—require a new approach to managing their accountability.

How often do you say you are going to do something or tell your team you want something done and everyone nods his or her head in agreement . . . but it doesn't get done? Action just seems to evaporate into thin air, right? The failure to complete tasks is at epidemic proportions in business. When what you set out to do falls off the radar for any number of "reasonable" reasons, you set the stage for a new cycle of apathy and cynicism. Unless you attach your commitments to a system that ensures their existence, you will pile up a stack of broken promises that guarantees you will not see your strategy executed—by you or anyone else.

Managing others often is designed to keep certain uncomfortable circumstances, issues, or problems in business from recurring. That's an easy pattern for most managers to fall into, and much of the time it involves avoiding a confrontation with employees.

I don't know too many people who relish confrontation unless they are narcissists and don't care what people think of them. It happens to even the best managers with the very best of intentions, and managing this way causes more issues than it solves. It creates what we don't want in our organizations: more entitlement, more apathy, more cynicism, more inertia, and less accountability. It diverts people from the mission of the company, and it keeps managers and their teams focused on the wrong activities. It doesn't have to be this way.

The Accountability Scorecard™: Start a Conversation FOR Action

By using the Accountability Scorecard, you can build a simple management principle into your organization: **Stop talking about what you're going to do, start making authentic promises to take action—and then, take action.**

Business is a network of conversations, and the conversation that makes the most positive impact on a team committed to accomplishing a major goal is the Conversation for Action. **Conversations for Action** are the bread and butter of accountability. Notice it's a conversation *for* action and not *about* action. When you talk "about" what you're going to do, there is no intention to be *in action*. A Conversation *for* Action, however, calls people to *be in action*.

How often do you assume that "talking about" is the same as the action itself? It's easy to collapse the two into one, and many organizations are stuck in inertia as a result.

What are Conversations for Action? They are the spoken acts of making, managing, and keeping promises. Performance is dependent on keeping promises, and with the Accountability Scorecard (www.ThirteenersBook.com), we take it a couple of steps further by having team members journaling regularly for their promises and then tracking each individual's actions and their impact on the team's progress. We provide feedback so that progress is visible and directly and positively impacts performance.

The Five Steps to Effective Promise Management

Promises are critical assets that you need to manage as effectively as you manage other asset resources in your organization. Here's how:

1. **Make promises.** Make clear promises to take action and produce a result that will move you and the organization closer to annual and/or monthly goals.

4. **Publish promises.** Issue promises publicly so that everyone can see who's pulling his or her weight. Attach promises to something (like the Accountability Scorecard sheet) that's tangible and visible to everyone so there's no question that a promise was made. There are no hidden or side deals.

5. **Journal promises.** Keep a journal of promises so they don't disappear or go out of existence.

4. **Act on promises.** Complete promises on time to maintain integrity. If that doesn't happen, find out what's missing

that prevented the promise from being kept. No shaming should be done for nonfulfillment.

5. **Measure promises.** Feedback is the critical element of consistency and reinforcement.

It's simple: Say what you're promising to contribute to move the team closer to its agreed-upon goals; publish your promises where everyone can see them (on the office wall or on the online Accountability Scorecard); make periodic notes about your activities; take action on your promises; and report to your team or accountability manager about keeping your promises. Finally, assign a percentage-of-completion value to your actions, so everyone on the team knows and can see the weight you are pulling, with them, to achieve the agreed-upon results for your team and organization.

These actions are critical to building teams that operate productively and effectively. Once you've successfully managed the first promise to its conclusion, you should re-promise for the next needed action.

The Accountability Scorecard approach is beneficial to teams for the following reasons:

- Individuals can contribute meaningful actions to a team intention.

- Dashboard feedback graphics are used to show team progress.

- Each individual's performance contributes to the entire team's results.

What Is Required for Effective Team Accountability?

When you're *in action* on your promises, you're being accountable, and your goal must be to get all your team members to be accountable as well. To achieve that goal, all you need is each individual's stated commitment to the team that he or she is willing to be held accountable and will use the simple tools needed to manage his or her promises.

As for yourself—the team leader—here's the key to achieving accountability: **Stop managing people. Start managing promises.**

Promises are your currency of action. Anything else is not worth the paper it is printed on. If you're responsible for getting things done through other people, scorecarding your promises will help you manage promises effectively.

It is critical to organizational performance to get everyone on the team engaged and aligned with the right effort. With the Accountability Scorecard, everyone on the team sees and knows what everyone else on the team is committed to and is taking action to accomplish. This is the most powerful energy you can create for your team and your organization. When everyone is engaged in promising and measuring, *unprecedented results* are not just a new possibility—they will be a new reality.

Seven Deadly Sins of Accountability

As you move forward, also be aware that organizations encounter seven classic pitfalls when inventing accountability. Be on the lookout for these:

1. Having too many goals

2. Not requiring promises from employees for how and when goals will be achieved

3. Not being aligned with the goals employees are working on

4. Not assigning champions for goals

5. Coming off your stand for employees' greatness and not expecting that they can accomplish impossible goals

6. Allowing conditional goal setting (e.g., "I can get this done if you can do this for me")

7. Allowing goals that are neither understandable nor measurable—goals that you will never be able to tell if they are actually completed

Accountability Is Up to You

Remember, once you have a commitment to a promise to take action, that promise becomes an asset to your organization. If you fail to complete the promise, the impact can be as damaging to the bottom line as if you had failed to manage any of the financial or other capital assets of your organization. You wouldn't waste the assets on your balance sheet, so why would you waste your promises?

Access to the action of accountability is through speaking, so a promise is a spoken act. It's an act that calls you to be, so it's a very important and distinct conversation. You can't give someone accountability, even if you're the supervisor or owner of the company.

Accountability is something you declare you are taking on because *you said* you were taking it on, not because someone else is demanding that you do so. People can make requests all day, and you can accept those requests. But unless you determine that you are going to be accountable for the action you have promised, no one can give you accountability for anything. Accountability is up to you.

STOP MANAGING PEOPLE.

Start Managing Your True Assets That Will Produce

Your Greatest Return On Investment:

START MANAGING PROMISES.

You can look at Stage Four on your downloaded Process Map.

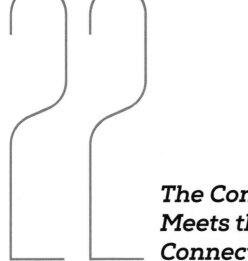

The Connected Leader Meets the Connected Company

{ *"All is connected . . . no one thing can change by itself."*

Paul Hawken }

What Do Connected Leaders and Connected Companies Look Like?

As you embark on making your company a THIRTEENER, you should have in your sights a vision of that goal. That is what you should be striving for.

The Unstoppable Leader's Manifesto

Leaders who end up building THIRTEENER companies use a distinctively different set of tools to create a profound connection with their employees and among their employees. They have learned to think differently about the conversations they participate in—with themselves and with others. They engage committed people and awaken them to the possibility of producing greater results. Employees who work for these astounding leaders know exactly what I am talking about.

These remarkable leaders have almost uncanny clarity about how human beings really think and act to produce results. They honor the perspectives of others and stand for people's remarkable desire to contribute to a vision they are completely connected to. Our business is to honor these leaders and teach others how to become as extraordinary as they are.

I have assembled the insights of those leaders into a manifesto of sorts—one that encapsulates the views and connected thinking of THIRTEENER leaders. I present this manifesto next. (You can also find it online at www.ThirteenersBook.com.) If you find it helpful, you can print it, have it enlarged, and hang it on your office wall.

The Connected Leader's Manifesto for THIRTEENERS

WE ASSERT:

1. Business is a community—a marketplace of human beings with a common, rightful, or proper concern or interest.

2. Human beings relate to each other in business within a unique network of conversations. Business is the network of conversations one chooses to engage in at work.

3. Human beings naturally desire a world that consists of a perspective of unlimited possibility. To invent such a world, the connected leader must be able to disengage from the past and imagine a future that the past says you can't achieve.

4. Connected leaders must work with their employees to reinvent the conversations in their business to create a new future.

5. Human beings in business usually operate with no awareness of the immense impact that negative, hidden conversations (that is, viral memes) have on business outcomes. Therefore, the leader must commit to uncovering his company's hidden viral memes.

6. Higher performance is possible only when positive conversations that make a difference are well communicated, clearly understood, and aligned with the purpose of the organization. Therefore, the connected leader must work with employees to create the positive conversations that will replace the negative viral memes within the organization.

7. Wherever there are secrets or anything that cannot be discussed at any level of the organization, you will find a seriously dysfunctional organization. Therefore, the connected leader must not keep secrets.

8. When employers pretend to be open or pretend to care, it undermines their relationships with employees. Therefore, connected leaders must "lead out loud" by showing vulnerability and asking all employees to contribute perspectives and ideas that will help the company succeed.

9. A connected leader must not let the past own the organization's future.

The Consciously Connected Leader

We live in the "Age of Connectedness" in business. Our challenge as connected leaders is to help our employees move from "unconscious disconnectedness" to "conscious connectedness." That is the job of the leader who wants to execute his or her strategy.

Unstoppable and connected leaders don't rely entirely on strategy to build their organizations; they leverage the principle of connectedness. Unconscious and disconnected leaders are reactive, behave automatically, and are at the mercy of circumstances they can't change. Consciously connected leaders act intentionally and cause things to happen to stay on purpose.

As a consciously connected leader, your objective is to transform your organization and your teams into a "connected culture" by bringing conscious connectedness to the execution of strategy.

At the core of transformation in your company is the transformation of yourself into a consciously connected leader.

What a Consciously Connected Leader Looks Like

Here are the key characteristics of the kind of leader you want to transform yourself into. A consciously connected leader

- **Supports the team and finds ways to remove barriers, so the team's work gets done faster and more effectively.** As a consciously connected leader, you make your team your priority. Your job is to allow people to struggle to discover solutions under your guidance and coaching. Never hand them "ready-to-wear" solutions that weaken your team's ability to think and solve problems. By doing this, you'll have the ability to take a vacation once in a while, knowing that you're leaving your organization in good hands.

- **Helps subordinates discover something for themselves and in the process become bigger (not smaller).** As a consciously connected leader, whenever you engage in a conversation with subordinates, never diminish them for their perspectives. Ask them first what they think would be a good approach to solving whatever issue they bring to you, and in this way, help them develop their thinking and rely on their own cognitive abilities, rather than react with thoughts that ultimately undermine their view of you, the company, and the situation they find themselves in. The latter can be the breeding ground for new negative memes.

- **Knows that benevolence goes a helluva long way.** Arrogance, or an attitude of "I've been through this before, and why can't you 'get it'?" won't help a company become unstoppable, so the consciously connected leader makes it safe for employees to say whatever they need to say. Giving employees the opportunity to contribute virtually assures that they will become unstoppable.

- **Never dismisses anyone from employment without first understanding and working through the core source of why that person is struggling.** Often the leader simply needs to look in the mirror to discover the problem.

- **Doesn't shy away from setting unreasonable goals.** If goals are reasonable, people will only make a little extra effort—but if goals are unreasonable, people will make real changes in the way they work. Consciously connected leaders don't play small.

- **Continues to look at the whole while making decisions that will only impact one area.** For example, when you change things in the call center, don't be blind to the impact that change will have on other parts of the organization.

- **Knows that success is not always about financial results.** When people make suggestions, a consciously connected leader tracks what happens to that suggestion and turns it into a promise that is followed up on with action. A consciously connected leader then reviews the action when it is completed with those to whom the leader made the promise.

- **Always assembles the right people to get the job done.**

- **Trusts his or her employees because they are the ones closest to customers.** Don't assume that you are the one with the best ideas and that employees don't have the same interest in success that you do.

- **Doesn't try to do it all.** Remember that it is your job to help people grow. If people aren't stretched, given the opportunity to make mistakes, and allowed to recognize their mistakes and make corrections, they will end up resenting you and will wait until you tell them what to do before they will do it.

- **Never criticizes employees in front of others (either in person or via the kind of email takedowns that some people have a hard time resisting), whether they are direct reports or not.** You're all on the same side with the same goals, so instead of pointing out employees' failures, you should ask them what they need from you to be able to accomplish what they promised or are responsible for. Criticism is judgment—and critical judgment is a major disconnector—so a consciously connected leader finds a better way to offer insight and mentoring.

- **Acts with speed to allow employees to see that things are happening, and acknowledges the source of the idea, giving all the credit away.** When you take the input of employees, that's the leader's job: to acknowledge and appreciate people's contributions. A consciously connected leader never withholds approval; that behavior is the chief cause of employees' committing acts of sabotage.

- **Gets people to make promises, and holds people accountable.** If you let your employees off the hook, they will think of you as weak and will lose respect for you.

- **Measures the keeping of promises.** Measurement creates the tension that makes the conversation for action more urgent. Action on promises is what moves a company forward to achieving greater heights.

- **Empowers the leader of problem-solving workouts to make decisions—on the spot—and then elicit commitments from people with "by when's" (a date by which something is promised) to see them completed.**

- **Knows that employees aren't perfect.** You should let them fail and then help them up. You don't have all the answers, and you know that your employees are eager to contribute.

- **Knows it is critical to remove old ideas and thinking from the company.** A consciously connected leader knows that the problem is never how to get new, innovative ideas and thinking into the company but how to get the old ideas and thinking out.

- **Takes past performance (his or her own) out of the possible future.** The past is of little use, and that includes the past experiences you have had with the people in your organization. People do not have a chance to produce great results if they feel defined by your narrow, rigid opinion of them based on their past results.

What a Consciously Connected Company Looks Like

A consciously connected company (a THIRTEENER) has consciously connected employees. These employees are connected to the company's vision, comprehend the opportunities that are available to them and for the future of the organization, have a clear understanding of what mission-critical actions are needed to achieve those opportunities, and will execute the organization's agreed-upon strategy. If you have consciously connected employees, you have the makings of a consciously connected business culture, one in which employees have a passionate commitment to each other and to the company's vision.

A Real-Life Story

Connectedness is not as abstract as you might initially think. There are important principles that anyone can use to create a Culture of Connectedness. Leaders and their teams who follow the principles and practices of the ConnectionPoints™ Promise-Based Strategy and Execution Management System end up with connected companies that produce amazing results. Here are some examples of the results of this process.

A few years ago, a very generous client of mine (whose company became a THIRTEENER) surprised me with an article that employees had written together describing what it was like to go through the ConnectionPoints process with me. Here are some excerpts from that article:

> "Alignment, motivation, healthier employee morale, and an improved bottom line—these are just a few of the exciting results of executing a strategic plan … [We] accepted this challenge and opened [our] minds to the possibilities … the possibilities of success, growth, greatness, and profound achievement!

> "The process began with a declaration of what our Group wanted their next 12 months to look like and the accomplishments we wanted to make as a team. Each team member, including the managing director, chose a 'role' that he or she would focus on and for which each person was individually accountable during the upcoming months.

> "This gave each member a sense of belonging, a sense of appreciation, and a defined place to contribute, as well as a voice in the decision-making process—all in an effort to

create a highly effective team where amazing results can flourish.

"This alignment, which was created by making sure all team members were engaged in the process and on the same page, has **catapulted [our] Group into a 60 percent increase in revenues in just the first five months** [their emphasis] of the program! Imagine what seven more months can do!"

To add to this story, the team had been struggling to gain traction for some time. Not only were they looking to increase the bottom line— they wanted to make sure they had the "right people on the bus," and they very importantly wanted to reduce a very alarming 30 percent write-off of client fees year to date.

In this five-month period and over the next seven months, they not only increased their revenue performance as they noted, but they reduced their 30 percent fee write-offs to less than 5 percent—which is much lower than the standard in their industry.

Here is what they individually had to say about the process as owners of the outcome. I tell you this not to toot my own horn but to demonstrate what real people did with the work they were challenged to do. After all, I didn't do the work—they did. I simply led them in the thinking and actions that helped them create a cogent Breakthrough Solutions Framework. Notice how they communicate the salient impact the system had on each of them and how, in the end, the process turned them into a highly conscious and connected team:

"Team alignment is one of the most powerful mechanisms a company can use to reach its strategic goals. Our program has given us the tools to reach alignment with one another, which includes support from all team members, as well as focusing our energy and resources on the desired outcome. As such, we see the connection between what we do and the success of our group, which the financial numbers have proven." —*Senior Consultant*

"I have learned what it means to draw on the individual strengths of group members, identify improvement opportunities, establish individual and group goals, and how to come into alignment to excel and achieve those goals. It has been a fun and fascinating experience to witness such a diverse group as ours working together as a team, appreciating what each of us brings to the team as we strive to become an example to the firm and marketplace of what is possible." —*Manager*

"What I've enjoyed most about [Dan Prosser's system] is the process itself. Team members at all levels are participating in decision making. When we started, many were apprehensive, and although it was brought to the forefront early that everyone wanted better communication, everyone was slow in opening up to express their thoughts. It took time to open up, but through the nonthreatening environment in which our meetings are held, better communication started happening.

From the very first day, everyone had a voice in determining our "guidelines" and establishing our "goals." Each person selected the goal that he or she wanted to "champion" and then also had a voice in determining the "action steps" to achieve a particular goal.

I've enjoyed seeing our team members step up and voice their opinion, determine the action steps to reach goals, follow through, and be held accountable to either achieve the action step or answer the question, "What was missing?" I feel the process is helping each member of the team grow, become more confident, and develop professionally. As each team member grows and strengthens, so does our entire team." —*Senior Manager*

"Dan Prosser transformed our limiting thinking from being a group of "bean counters" to being value-added professionals that are the catalyst for change in our clients' businesses. Once the group declared that this was the way we wanted to view ourselves and be viewed by the marketplace and our partners, amazing things started to happen. A new energy and focus entered the group, and the tide started to change. From that point forward, anything that did not look like truly professional, high-quality work or thinking stood out as not being in alignment with our core values. The biggest beneficiaries of this change have been our clients. We are making more and better recommendations to our clients, and in turn, we are helping them achieve more in their business." —*Managing Director*

"To produce outstanding results much like the [group], consider that business is simply a network of conversations; it is a choice between positive or negative dialogues. The power comes from choosing to invent new ones that inspire a group of people to be extraordinary and do extraordinary things.

According to Dan Prosser, 'For a company to truly "work," people have to change the conversations that are stopping or slowing them down into conversations that make a difference for everyone involved: owner, employee, customer, supplier and community.'" —*Senior Consultant*

This organization has invented a new way of thinking, a new way of being. It is proof that true greatness comes when minds think alike and energies are focused toward the same objective.

The difference that was made wasn't just the sum of the pieces that they assembled to accomplish their outstanding outcome. It came as a result of the profound conscious connectedness they created among themselves, with their vision of the organization, through their values, and finally with the future they had envisioned for themselves.

This is what a consciously connected THIRTEENER organization looks like, and this is what happens when an organization rigorously follows the ConnectionPoints system to execute a strategy that would never have happened on its own.

NOTES

1. Ben Casselman, "Risk-Averse Culture Infects U.S. Workers, Entrepreneurs," *Wall Street Journal*, June 2, 2013, http://online.wsj.com/news/articles/SB1000 14241278873240314045 78481162903760052/.

2. Ben Casselman, "The Slow Death of American Entrepreneurship," FiveThirtyEightEconomics, May 15, 2014, http://fivethirtyeight.com/features/the-slow-death-of-american -entrepreneurship/.

3. Brené Brown, PhD, LMSW, is a research professor at the University of Houston Graduate College of Social Work. She has spent the past dozen years or so studying vulnerability, courage, worthiness, and shame. She is the author of the book *Daring Greatly: How the Courage to Be Vulnerable Transforms the Way We Live, Love, Parent, and Lead.* She has appeared at TED and TEDxHouston events; on Oprah's *Super Soul Sunday* program; and on PBS, NPR, and CNN. Her articles have appeared in the *Washington Post* and *Psychology Today*, among other media outlets. Her work includes some of the best insights I've ever seen into why so many businesses fail at executing their strategy. Suddenly, the issue of toxic workplaces, shame, and the havoc it wreaks in organizations is going mainstream. I couldn't be more pleased.

4. Kim Marquis, "Summit County Snowboarders Ride Away with $3,600 Prize," *SummitDaily*, November 14, 2004.

5. Leon Lederman with Dick Teresi, *The God Particle: If the Universe Is the Answer, What Is the Question?* (New York: Dell, 1993).

6. Edward M. Hallowell and Michael G. Thompson, *Finding the Heart of the Child* (Braintree, MA: Association of Independent Schools in New England, 1993), 193–209.

7. Richard Dawkins, *The Selfish Gene: The Thirtieth Anniversary Edition* (Oxford, England: Oxford University Press, 2006), 192. Originally published in 1976.

8. Christine Porath and Christine Pearson, "The Price of Incivility," *Harvard Business Review* (January–February 2013), http://hbr.org/2013/01/the-price-of-incivility/.

9. Ibid.

10. Dan Dennett, "Dangerous Memes," Filmed Feb. 2002, TED talks video, 15:26, http://www.ted.com/talks/dan_dennett_on_dangerous_memes.

11. Ibid.

12. Joel Arthur Barker, *Paradigms: The Business of Discovering the Future* (New York: Harper Business, 1992), 140.

13. Peter Block, *Stewardship: Choosing Service over Self-Interest* (San Francisco, CA: Berrett-Koehler, 1993), 35.

14. Howard Phillips Lovecraft, *Supernatural Horror in Literature* (New York: Dover, 1973).

15. Richard T. Pascale, Mark Milleman, and Linda Gioja, *Surfing the Edge of Chaos: The Laws of Nature and the New Laws of Business* (New York: Crown, 2000).

16. Dee Hock, *Birth of the Chaordic Age* (San Francisco, CA: Berrett-Koehler, 2000).

17. G. Nicolis and I. Prigogine, *Exploring Complexity: An Introduction* (New York: W. H. Freeman, 1989).

18. Donald Sull, *Why Good Companies Go Bad and How Great Managers Remake Them* (Boston: Harvard Business School Press, 2005).

19. Joel Arthur Barker, *Paradigms: The Business of Discovering the Future* (New York: Harper-Collins, 1992).

20. D. L. Cooperrider and D. Whitney, "Appreciative Inquiry: A Positive Revolution in Change," in *The Change Handbook*, ed. Peggy Holman and Tom Devane (San Francisco: Berrett-Koehler, 1999), 245–263.

"Success is not final, failure is not fatal: it is the courage to continue that counts"

– Winston Churchill

THIRTEENERS

EXTRAS

Thank you for buying THIRTEENERS

As a "thank you" we've got some added extras for you in
addition to the downloads mentioned within the book.
Just visit us at www.ThirteenersBook.com

---

*If there is any way we can help you achieve your vision to
become a THIRTEENER please call us.
You can reach the author personally by email at:
info@ThirteenersBook.com*

Wishing you success in taking your organization to a new
level as you become a THIRTEENER!

Dan Prosser

HAVE
DAN PROSSER
SPEAK

Dan Prosser is available for Keynote presentations and Workshops as well as CEO mentoring and Team consulting.

Sitting through strategic planning sessions is often boring with only mediocre or short-lived results to show for all the work. What would you want to build if you knew your team could not fail?

Dan Prosser's **ConnectionPoints**™ Promise-Based Strategy and Execution system helps CEOs and their teams uncover the very thing that prevents over 87% of companies from executing their strategy.

Dan Prosser makes understanding transformation for your organization fun and easy. His deep-dive delivery style along with humor, stories, simple illustrations, and interactive activities, keeps his audiences engaged and informed.

For more Information, visit
ThirteenersBook.com